T0161490

FINANCE YOUR OWN BUSINESS

GET ON THE FINANCING FAST TRACK

GARRETT SUTTON, ESQ.
GERRI DETWEILER

Published by SuccessDNA, an imprint of Brisance Books Group LLC

Success DNA, Inc.
2248 Meridian Boulevard, Suite H.
Minden, Nevada 89423

Printed in the United States of America

First Edition: 2015

ISBN: 978-1-944194-01-7

Acknowledgements

The authors would like to thank the following people for their insights and contributions to this book: Dave Archer, Grayson Bell, Libby Bierman, Robin Bramman, Ali Brown, John Cambier, Adam Cohen, Aaron and Kathy Corr, Jan Davis, Jeff Desich, Chris Kelley, Levi King, Shaun Merriman, Julia Pimsleur, Mark Pinskey, Emily Chase Smith, Tom Trafficante, Claudia Viek, Brian Ward, Michael Weiss, and Tom Wheelwright.

Your assistance is greatly appreciated.

Books by the Authors

Garrett Sutton

Start Your Own Corporation

Run Your Own Corporation

The ABCs of Getting out of Debt

Writing Winning Business Plans

Buying & Selling a Business

Loopholes of Real Estate

How to Use Limited Liability Companies and Limited Partnerships

Gerri Detweiler

Debt Collection Answers: How to Use Debt Collection Laws to Protect Your Rights

Reduce Debt, Reduce Stress: Real Life Solutions for Solving Your Credit Crisis

The Ultimate Credit Handbook

Invest In Yourself: Six Secrets to a Rich Life

Contents

Foreword

By Ali Brown

When I started my business in New York in 1999, I was broke. My credit was terrible, and I had tons of debt. But it didn't stop me. In fact, I believe it helped propel me to success. Why? Because I had no other choice. Not only did I want to make money fast, I needed to!

And that drive led me to an incredibly successful entrepreneurial career as well as an Inc 500 ranked enterprise sharing leadership and business strategies with other women business owners.

By definition, entrepreneurs are risk takers. Just by picking up this book, I know something about you: You have dreams that are probably much bigger than your bank account. You know you are more than your credit score. And you are ready to turn your dreams into reality no matter what "they" say.

You don't have to get a small business loan to start a business, but there are times when access to credit can be an asset. If you are going to get a loan or raise money through crowdfunding, you want to be smart about it. And that's what this book will help you do.

Since launching my business over fifteen years ago, I've had the privilege to work with thousands of entrepreneurs from all kinds of backgrounds. One thing I've learned and share with them is that it is critical to have mentors and coaches; smart people who can help you fill in the gaps and avoid pitfalls.

Garrett Sutton is one of those people in my network. He's a corporate attorney with a passion for helping entrepreneurs. With his co-author Gerri Detweiler, a nationally recognized credit expert, he has created this guide to help you navigate the sometimes rough waters of financing a business.

If you are like me, you aren't willing to wait until conditions are perfect for starting your business. You want to dive in *now*. *Finance Your Own Business* will give you lots of strategies for raising the money you need to get off the ground or take your business to the next level. I wish I had this kind of information when I got started!

~Ali Brown, Leading Entrepreneur, Mentor, Angel Investor, www.AliBrown.com

Part One: Finding Financing

Overview

A Tale of Two Business Start Ups

Mike, Jan and Liz had worked their way up the ladder at the PR firm where they landed after college.

Talented and hardworking, they loved their jobs in the beginning. But as the company grew and they moved up the ranks, they found themselves in endless meetings, scheduling more endless meetings. When a much larger agency acquired the firm, they pictured more endless meetings. All three of them decided to take their severance money and pursue other opportunities.

Starting with his $50,000 severance pay Mike built his PR firm into a boutique agency billing over $5 million a year. Creative and personable, Mike's reputation and company grew quickly. As it did, he found himself constantly putting out fires—and all too often, they were financial fires.

Many of his clients were Fortune 500 companies that paid well, but slowly. Sometimes, it took six months to collect from them. The larger the client company, it seemed, the longer it took to get paid. In the meantime, he had to keep paying salaries and overhead. More than once, he threw expenses onto his personal credit cards. And he missed a payment more than once because he was too busy to notice when the bills were due. His interest rates on his credit cards were now all in the double digits.

One day, Mike was contacted by a company that told him they could factor his firm's receivables. The pitch was attractive: Get paid for work right away, and let someone else worry about collecting on the invoice. The cut he had to give the factoring firm shaved a little more off his already thin margins, but at least he was making payroll.

Then the bank where he held his business accounts, including his operating line of credit, was sold. The line of credit—his lifeline—was cut, because he didn't meet the new bank's credit criteria. Now he didn't have the funds he needed to float him between client payments, and it looked like his business might not make it. In his moment of desperation, he received a call from one of the bigger firms. They were looking for companies to acquire and were interested in his.

Like Mike, Jan and Liz joined together to start their own PR firm at the same time. They each took $15,000 from their severance pay and parked the $30,000 in their business bank accounts, agreeing not to spend it except in an absolute emergency. Both women had excellent credit ratings, and wanted to keep them strong. On advice from their CPA, they carefully researched the business credit building process so they wouldn't run into the cash flow problems the CPA had seen so many of his clients encounter.

Their firm also grew, but they watched their expenses like hawks, reviewed their finances every week, and avoided tapping their personal credit. When Jan and Liz needed computers and a phone system for their small office, they leased them. When they needed office supplies, they charged them to their office supply account and paid them off when they came due.

Many of the accounts they established allowed them to pay in 30, 60, and sometimes 90 days. Whenever possible, they chose accounts with companies that gave them the longest terms, and once their firm established a payment history, they negotiated even better terms. They also established an operating line of credit at their bank, but used very little of it.

Unlike Mike, who hired the best and the brightest, Jan and Liz outsourced a lot of their work to avoid a large payroll. Several of their best employees agreed to work on more modest salaries, but with a generous bonus plan at the end of the year based on the firm's profits. They, too, were billing several million dollars a year when they received a call from the larger firms.

How Deep Is Your Well?

Mike's story is a common one, except that the vast majority don't survive the financial turbulence that Mike and his business faced. Entrepreneurs are usually self-starters who are good at what they know. They come up with great concepts, invest in marketing and advertising, and are willing to work hard to get the job done. But ultimately, they fail because they never planned for their capital needs. Think of capitalizing business as digging a well. Smart business owners dig the well as deep as possible—or at least lay that groundwork for doing so. Otherwise, they are constantly trying to refill the well every time it stops raining business.

The biggest tragedy is that many business owners wait until it is too late to start digging that well; that is, looking for capital. At that point, like Mike, they usually end up out of luck. The reality is, no one wants to give you money if they know you need it. Word to the wise: Dig your well when you don't need the water.

What is Financing a Business?

This is a book about financing your business. It is not about business finance. What is the difference? Business finance is the broad activity of managing money and other assets within a company. Business finance courses in college and in graduate school deal with accounting methods, strategic investing, debt management and financial principles. You will often hear people say, "He's a finance guy." Or "She's a financial whiz." These are people who know how to manage, move and manipulate money to the company's (and their) benefit.

Financing a business, though it sounds similar, is not the same thing. Instead, it means bringing money into your business. It's a much narrower activity than business finance, certainly for young businesses. But it is arguably a more important activity. You can hire the finance guy to manage all the money later. But first you need to get started and you need money to do it. And then you need to keep going—and unless your business is rolling in cash, you need the continuing financing to grow it.

As a corporate attorney, Garrett Sutton, one of the authors of this book, has worked with business owners all over the world, at all stages of their businesses—from start-up to selling the business. But one thing he hears time and time again is that business owners are frustrated when it comes to getting the financing they need to either start a venture or to grow it. They often don't realize the variety of financing options available to them, and as a result may wind up with the wrong kind of financing. We don't want that to happen to you.

As a credit expert, Gerri Detweiler, the other author of this book, has heard too many stories from entrepreneurs who have destroyed their personal credit because they didn't understand how to protect themselves. They found themselves dealing with the aftermath of their credit decisions for many years. And that includes successful business owners as well as those whose ventures failed! We don't want that to happen to you either.

Businesses need financing for a variety of reasons, including:

- To start up
- To expand and grow
- To develop new products
- To enter new markets
- To acquire other businesses

Where Does The Money Come From?

Every year, *Inc.* magazine publishes the Inc. 500 issue, which features 500 of the fastest growing private companies in America. It's fascinating to see all the different types of businesses featured, and how they are growing.

In that issue, Inc. also publishes a survey of the ways these companies access start-up capital. In one issue, those top ways were:

- Personal savings (71%)
- Loans from friends and family (21%)
- Personal bank loans (13%)
- Home equity loans or lines of credit (12%)
- Angel funding (9%)
- Venture capital (6%)
- SBA loans (3%)

None reported tapping the fairly new, but soon-to-explode world of crowdfunding, which we shall discuss in Chapter 15.

Never Enough

Can you guess what these same entrepreneurs said was their biggest mistake or challenge their first year? That's right: Shortage of capital.

"One of the primary reasons why most businesses fail is a lack of available cash," warns Mitchell Weiss, a former financial services executive and the author of *Business Happens*. "People just starting out don't want to borrow or think about it. As lots of people know, you can get money when you don't need it and it's hard to get it when you do. You want a line of credit so you can tap it when you need it."

In this book we'll talk about the merits (and downsides) of many of these financing approaches and how you may be able to use them get the funding you need. We will also share some you may have not heard much about such as raising money from foreign investors seeking US visas, merchant cash advances and SBIR grants.

But we'll also talk about something you typically won't find in a business financing book: How these methods may affect your credit.

Starting a business is risky. You've seen the statistics about how many fail. But you wouldn't be reading this book if you aren't at least contemplating entrepreneurship. Our goal is to help you minimize the risks as much as possible. Starting a risk-free business isn't realistic. There are no guarantees in life. But learning how to minimize the risk to your personal credit and your personal assets will make it easier for you to weather the inevitable ups and downs.

In Part One we will discuss the various types of financing available to you.

In Part Two we will review the foundation you need to develop ongoing funding. Part Three will focus on the various ways to bring investors into your company. And in Part Four we're going to provide some caution and some strategies for success.

Let's get started.

Chapter 1

Popular Financing Strategies

It takes a lot to impress the "Sharks" on Shark Tank, the popular television show where entrepreneurs pitch their business ideas to successful millionaires and billionaires in hopes of bringing them on as investors and partners in their businesses. When 35-year-old Julie Busha shared her product line, Slawsa, a unique condiment that is a cross between salsa and coleslaw, the judges not only loved the taste but they were clearly impressed by the fact that she was willing and able to forgo a salary in order to funnel all sales proceeds into the growth of the company.

She was able to do that because she funded the company entirely from personal savings. In fact, when the opportunity came for her to buy Slawsa from her former partner, per his request, she was able to do so without getting a loan. She had set aside a nice nest egg from the decade she spent as a sports marketer, primarily in NASCAR, and says she dug into her savings to finance much of the start-up costs: production, travel to pitch retailers, marketing, legal costs and more. "It's not cheap to start a company, especially in an industry as highly competitive as the grocery one; it takes a special effort" she says.

Billionaire Shark Tank investor Mark Cuban was extremely supportive of Busha telling her "you're an example like we rarely have in here and I'll be a customer for life." Cuban also expanded after she left the room, "The fact that she scrimped, has no debt, pays off her credit cards, saved up enough money to invest into this company and buy him out is such an amazing example for everybody." Fellow Shark Robert Herjavec also shared supportive comments about Busha's work ethic.

When she secured a coveted spot on Shark Tank, Busha had to ramp up production to meet the expected demand the show would generate. She and her husband borrowed equity from their home to fund that. "It is easy?" she says. "No. But I'm not doing this because I think it will be."

Most Popular Financing Methods

The four most popular ways to finance a business are the ways you would expect: Personal savings, loans from friends and family, home equity loans and personal bank loans.

Let's review each one.

Personal Savings

Conceptually, it makes perfect sense that using your personal savings to start and finance your business is the first choice for entrepreneurs. There is no interest expense, no creditors wanting to be paid back and no awkwardness or embarrassment in asking others for money. You simply go to the bank and pull out your savings. (Hopefully, you are using a separate corporation or LLC and the money gets deposited into a separate business bank account.)

But in taking this very easy and rational step please ask yourself some equally rational questions:

1. Can I afford to lose all this money?
2. Do I understand that not every business succeeds?

3. How long will it take me to save this amount of money again?
4. How would a loss of this money affect my family?
5. Have I thought enough about alternative ways to finance the business?

In presenting these questions we are not trying to deter you from your goals. Instead, we want you to be realistic with them.

Most businesses need financing along the way. They need it at the start-up phase, the growth phase and all the other phases that occur during the life of an enterprise. If your personal savings can cover every phase, good for you. (You can stop reading now.) For most of us, we need to have alternative financing methods in mind. We need to keep reading this book. And by learning the various financing methods we then have to ask: Should I use up all of my personal savings to get the business going? Should I consider the other alternatives so that not all of my savings are at risk?

We should also clarify what we mean by personal savings. They do not include money in retirement accounts. Your IRA and 401(k) are savings for your sunset years. They are usually protected from creditors and the bankruptcy courts. Pulling these monies out of a protected retirement account (which can incur large penalties and fees if done wrong) may be a very bad move. If your retirement age is nearing and you don't have enough time to rebuild depleted accounts, it could be disastrous.

Beware of charlatans on the internet claiming you can easily use your retirement money to start a business. These firms tell you that by using a self-directed IRA or a special 401(k) you can easily use your retirement funds to invest in your own business. But what they don't tell you is that the IRS has strict rules regarding such transactions. We will discuss these issues further in Chapter 6.

The bigger point here is that whether it is your personal savings or retirement savings, you may not want to go all in. You may want to use other proven strategies to finance your business or real estate investment.

Let's consider the second most popular method.

Friends and Family

Friends and family have always been a great source for boot strap financing. Friends and family want you to succeed and are a lot more likely to take a chance on you than any bank would. That personal belief in you, that personal connection, is a special bond. Be very careful about testing it with a business transaction.

Your relationships are more important than your business. We start with that premise. Accordingly, many seasoned entrepreneurs advise others to never accept money from friends and family. Their take is that if your idea has merit you can find an angel investor and avoid testing a personal relationship altogether. Friends and family members have lost money in the past and will do so in the future. Do you want to be the one to have to confront it every Thanksgiving?

You have to ask yourself that same question. It is gut check time. This type of financing is often called the "family, friends and fools" approach. We don't want you to be the fool for taking money from family and friends that may never be repaid— you may never hear the end of it.

Alright, now that you are sufficiently forewarned and prepared, let's discuss how to do it the right way. A huge amount of money is raised from friends and family for investments every year and not every Thanksgiving dinner is being ruined. Obviously, some people are doing it right.

Here are four tips to consider.

Understand Their Motivation

A large percentage of friends and family members' sole motivation is to help you out. They may not tell you this, and you can't assume it, but they may even consider their money to be a gift. That said, they may also see their extension of money as a reasonable investment. They believe in you and your project, and if a decent return comes with it, all the better. Ask yourself why they are investing, and tailor your approach to meet their needs.

A key in this is knowing when to say "No." Within your reservoir of goodwill are some people who will help you to their own detriment. If a friend or family member really can't afford to help you, don't even ask.

Be Honest and Transparent

Make sure they know the risks of the investment before you take their money. Explain that not only are you not likely to become the next Google but that they may actually lose their entire investment. Make sure that the money they are providing is money they can afford to lose.

While this may not sound like a very positive conversation to have when everyone is charged up to conquer the world, it is a necessary step. Your supporters will appreciate your candor, and may even continue to socialize with you if things don't go well.

Consider Taking Money As A Loan

You don't always have to sell equity in your company. It may be appropriate to borrow the money from friends and family. You promise to pay it back, with interest. And then you do so. Most businesses offer no liquidity, meaning it is very difficult to cash out an equity investment. So even if the business survives your friends' money is stuck in the investment. By borrowing the money and paying it back, your supporters have helped you get started and you are square with them.

Interestingly enough, friends and family may be more pie in the sky about this investment than you are. They may have visions of $1,000 turning into $1,000,000. You have to be the adult. A loan may be the safer course for them and you need to tell them so. If they really want equity in the company they can buy in at a later round when things are hopefully more stable.

Get Everything in Writing

Be sure to put the terms of your agreement in writing. If it is a loan, a promissory note with an interest rate and payment time frames should be drafted. If it is an equity investment the terms must be spelled out with specificity. The assistance of an attorney is strongly suggested. Be sure that all parties agree to all the important terms and details and then sign and save the agreement.

Many people lament the end of the handshake deal. They ask why everything has to be in writing nowadays. And the answer is because our lives have become too over stimulated with computers, smartphones and television. We are constantly bombarded with new information, new things to process and new distractions. As a result, to expect two people to remember exactly the terms of a handshake deal that was agreed to even two months ago is almost quaint. Certainty is found in well-drafted written documents. This rule applies for all financing methods discussed from here on in.

There's another reason why putting this agreement in writing is so important: the IRS. If your business doesn't succeed, your lender may be able to deduct the losses from the loan. But if there is nothing in writing and no repayment schedule, fat chance that will happen. And it gets worse: the IRS may treat the money they lent or invested as a gift, which if the amount is large can create gift tax issues.

Next, we'll talk about another popular method of business financing that will most certainly involve a contract.

Tapping Home Equity

Just a few years ago, home equity loans were one of the easiest ways to finance a business. Home values were high and lender requirements were lax. That changed dramatically when the housing boom turned to bust. With less equity and much more stringent underwriting by lenders it's harder to turn your equity into start-up capital.

But these loans haven't gone away entirely. Seventeen percent of businesses with less than $100,000 in sales use home equity lines of credit for business purposes, according to Barlow Research's Small Office/Home Office Opportunity study.

There are several ways to use home equity to borrow for your business:

- A home equity loan or line of credit
- Refinance your current mortgage for more than you owe, and take cash out for your business
- Pledge home equity as part of an SBA loan or other small business loan

We'll talk about the latter option—SBA and small business loans—in Chapters 3 and 4. Here we will focus on the first two options.

As mentioned, it is much harder to qualify for mortgages, including home equity loans, than it was prior to the housing downturn. You'll generally only be able to borrow up to 80% of your home's appraised value, minus any first mortgage.

Your personal credit score will be a key factor in determining which program you qualify for, and the rate you'll pay. Make sure you check your credit reports at AnnualCreditReport.com at least six weeks before applying for one of these loans, to give yourself time to fix mistakes. While you're at it, check your credit score for free at Credit.com to get an understanding of where you stand. Keep in mind, though, that for mortgage applications, lenders use a specific version of the FICO score which they will obtain with your credit reports from each of the three major credit bureaus. The middle of the three scores that are returned will usually be used for qualification purposes. You can learn more about credit scores in the 2012 edition of Garrett Sutton's *The ABC's Of Getting Out of Debt* (We will refer to several of Garrett's books throughout the text. Of course, not every related topic can be included in just one book. So the idea is to provide you with an easy reference point for more information.)

Don't quit your day job just yet! If you are still working a full-time job, apply for a home equity loan or line of credit while you can still show steady employment. Lenders want to see two years of documented income, and it's become more challenging for those who are self-employed to get these loans. Unless your spouse can qualify for the loan on his or her income and credit score alone, it's best to get a loan nailed down before go out on your own.

Home equity loans or lines of credit, as well as "cash-out refi's" may be available from your local bank or credit union, a megabank, online lender or mortgage broker. Shop around by contacting several lenders or using an online portal, or by hiring a mortgage broker to shop for you. Just try to limit applications to a two-week period to avoid possible damage to your credit score that can result from multiple inquiries. (Mortgage-related inquiries within a 14 or 45 day stretch will usually be counted as one, depending on which credit scoring model is used.)

What's the downside of using home equity to start your venture? The loan will be reported on your personal credit reports and can affect your credit scores. If you pay those loans on time, however, it shouldn't create too much of a problem. But if you fall behind on a payment on any mortgage loan—home equity or otherwise—your credit scores will likely plummet, at least in the short term.

Another consideration to keep in mind is the fact that home equity lines of credit typically offer interest-only payments for an initial period, called the "draw" period, which usually lasts for ten years, though sometimes it is shorter or longer. After that period, the borrower can no longer borrow against the line of credit, and must pay the entire loan back—interest plus principal—over a set period of time, which may be 10, 15 or 25 years, depending on the terms of the loan. During this latter period, the monthly payment will likely be substantially higher than during the draw period. So it is crucial to understand the term of the loan and what kinds of payments will be required during that time or you may find yourself in default, or forced to sell your home to pay back the loan.

If you're thinking of taking out one of these loans, one of the hardest things to do it so put your optimism aside for a moment. Most entrepreneurs are risk-takers; if they weren't, they'd never venture out on their own. But you need to think about what will happen if it takes longer to get off the ground than you planned. Will you be able to repay the loan? What happens if you can't?

How Long Is Your Runway?

Emily Chase Smith is an attorney and coach who works with entrepreneurs. She says: "Every business takes twice as much time and twice as much money as you think it will, and we call that your runway. You want to extend your runway as far as you possibly can. Sometimes as small business owners, we just see the vision so clearly, so we go for the big vision and we don't have a plan for how we're going to get there. So we might go out and rent a giant office because that's our vision. We're going to have this fantastic law firm or we're going to have this great retail space, to satisfy our vision as opposed to taking the realistic steps to get there. But then we run out of runway. We run out of money and run out of time. Perhaps (if we took it more slowly) we could have had a fantastic business."

Reverse Mortgages

If you are 62 years or older and you have equity in your home, you may want to consider a reverse mortgage (officially known as a home equity conversion mortgage) instead of a home equity loan.

A reverse mortgage is a federally-insured mortgage, only available to homeowners 62 years or older. You get the proceeds of the loan in one of three ways; as a lump sum, in monthly installments or as you need it (a line of credit). You don't make mortgage payments, but you are required to pay your taxes and homeowners insurance. And if you get a reverse mortgage on a property that already has a mortgage, the existing loan will be paid off and a new loan put in place.

When you sell your home, or if you die before then, the reverse mortgage is paid off—including interest and fees that have accrued on the loan—and any equity left in the home goes to your heirs or estate. If your home's value has dropped, however, and there is not enough equity to pay off the reverse mortgage, then the lender takes the loss regardless of other assets you may leave behind.

The advantage of this type of mortgage for an entrepreneur is clear: If it takes you longer to generate cash flow than expected, you won't be scrambling to make payments on your mortgage or a home equity loan.

In the past, lenders didn't even look at borrower's credit reports, making these loans especially attractive to those with past credit problems. But due to losses by the FHA, a "financial review" that includes a credit check is required as of March 2015. That doesn't mean you can't get a reverse mortgage if you have bad credit, but it does mean you may need to provide an explanation for how you plan to use funds to pay back currently delinquent debts. Still, a reverse mortgage isn't reported on traditional credit reports, so taking one out won't hurt the business owner's credit history.

These loans can get expensive, and some older people have been sold loans that weren't appropriate for them. Of course, there is always the risk of sinking your home equity into a business venture that might fail. You can lose your equity and have nothing to show for it. As a result of past abuses in this industry, you are required to get mandatory counseling from a HUD-approved counselor before you can get one of these loans.

On the other hand, unlike a home equity loan, you won't be kicked out of your house because you can't make your loan payments. You must keep up with your property taxes and required assessments such as homeowner association dues, though, or you could lose your home. The lender will also require you to keep a minimum amount of homeowner insurance in force to protect the lender in case of a fire or other catastrophe. You will have to be able to document that you can afford to continue to make your insurance and tax payments in order to get one of these loans.

Personal Bank Loans

In the Inc. 500 survey, 13% of respondents said they used personal bank loans to fund their businesses. That makes sense, as it can be hard to get a business loan for a brand-new venture. However, personal loans also carry a tremendous about of risk.

Getting a personal loan will require a personal credit score strong enough to help you qualify for the loan, and a large and steady enough income to support the payments. If you are considering a personal loan for business financing, ask potential lenders the following questions:

Do you have a minimum credit score requirement? If the lender will tell you what the minimum credit score needed is in order to qualify, you'll at least know whether you are in the ballpark. Understand, though, that you don't have a single credit score; you have many. There is a good chance that if you checked your credit scores, you won't have seen the same exact credit score the lender is using. That's true even if you order your credit score from the same bureau the lender uses. Lenders may use custom scores, or scores that aren't generally available to consumers.

If you are turned down for a personal loan, the lender is required to disclose your actual credit score, based on the credit scoring model they used, and give you information about how to order a free copy of your credit report from the reporting agency that supplied your report. Take advantage of this opportunity to learn more about your credit score for free.

Is there a maximum debt-to-income ratio you'll accept? A debt-to-income ratio typically compares the borrower's gross (before tax) monthly income to monthly debt payments. A typical requirement for many lenders is that debt payments excluding any mortgage payment don't exceed 28 – 30% of gross income, and that total debt payments including a mortgage total no more than 38 – 40% of gross income. Be sure to count the new loan when calculating your debt-to-income ratio.

What are my payment options? Will you have a fixed monthly payment, or will you be able to make minimum monthly payments if cash flow is tight?

Is this a revolving or installment loan? With a revolving loan, you can borrow up to a certain limit (your credit line), while an installment loan will allow you to borrow a specific amount of money and pay it back over a specific period of time. These two types of loans are very different in terms of how they affect your personal credit scores.

Let's say you need a $10,000 loan to start your business. If you get a revolving line of credit and use $8000 right away, you are using 80% of your available credit. In credit scoring terms, that ratio of available credit to balance is called the "utilization" or "debt usage" ratio. And when it comes to your credit scores, that high utilization ratio is likely to hurt your credit scores. There's no ideal utilization ratio, but consumers with the highest credit scores tend to use about 10% of their available credit.

But if you get that same loan as an installment loan, then it will be viewed differently. If your loan is reported as "installment" rather than "revolving" credit, the amount of debt is part of the credit score calculation, but utilization is less likely to be a problem. You can shop for a personal loan to start your business by finding out what your current bank or credit union has to offer. One type of personal loan that is growing in popularity is the peer to peer, or P2P loan.

Peer to Peer Loans

The original premise behind peer to peer or "P2P" loans was to cut out the middleman—banks—and to match individuals who have money to lend (lenders/investors) with individuals who need to borrow money. The premise was that lender/investors can earn a better return on their money by lending directly. In addition, these companies sold lenders on the idea that they could spread out their risk by lending small amounts of money to many different borrowers. LendingClub.com and Prosper.com are two of the earliest major players in this space, and they have both been very successful with this model. So successful in fact, that it's no longer just individual lenders providing the funds for these loans. Large investors such as pension funds and institutional investors are major lenders for these platforms now, too.

Borrowers who qualify typically get a loan with a fixed interest rate and fixed monthly payments. Often these loans are used by individuals who are starting, or growing a business. If you are looking for a personal loan and have a good credit score, you may want to check out a P2P lender. It is expected that more lenders will get into this business as it grows in popularity. For more information on these lenders visit the Resource Section.

We will talk a bit more about these companies in Chapter 15, Crowdfunding.

But in chapter 2, let's investigate business plastic…

Chapter 2

Business Credit Cards

Grayson Bell comes from an entrepreneurial family, and after seeing his parents and brother succeed in their ventures, he decided to launch his own business while still in college. He already had two personal credit cards, and had started to fall into the trap of paying only the minimum payment after an expensive car repair had left him owing more than he could repay in a month. His hope was that his business could help him pay down his credit card debt.

After some careful research, he decided to start an online electronics store. And to fund it he turned to credit cards. As he describes it on his website, DebtRoundUp.com:

"One factor of marketing that I learned really quick is that it costs money to do quality marketing. I took a lot of time to create free marketing buzz, but in order to get the customers that I needed to succeed, I needed to spend money on marketing. Since I didn't have any money, my credit card became my business loan. Soon, I found out that I would need another credit card to continue with my marketing plan. Another credit card added to the bunch put my total to three; two of which were close to being maxed out."

Four years into his business, Grayson decided to close it. At that point he had nearly $50,000 in credit card debt. Eventually, he was able to pay that all back without filing for bankruptcy or ruining his credit rating, and he shares how he did that on his blog. But he warns others about going down the road he went down. "The main thing I learned was to never, ever use a credit card to start and run a business," he says.

Not all stories end like Grayson's. Some businesses funded with plastic succeed. Others fail, and their owners wind up in bankruptcy. His is a cautionary tale, though, for those who might be tempted to just charge their start-up expenses and worry about how to pay them later.

When the US General Accounting Office submitted a report to Congress on the use of small business credit cards, it said that "the vast majority of small businesses use personal or small business credit cards." At the time the GAO conducted its research (the end of 2009), it found that 83 percent of small businesses used credit cards. Of that number 64 percent used small business cards, and 41 percent used personal cards.

Starting out, entrepreneurs usually have two choices: to use personal credit cards for business purposes, or to get a small business credit card. Whichever route you decide to go, one of the most important things you can do is to make sure you have a credit card that you use strictly for business purposes. That means you should not put any personal purchases on this card.

There are three good reasons for this:

- It can make your life much simpler come tax time. Your accountant will be able to easily identify your business purchases, and be able to make sure that you get the appropriate deductions.
- It may save you money at tax time. If you use your card strictly for business purposes, you may be able

to deduct the interest, annual fee, and other fees. This is much harder to do if you mix business and personal purchases on the same card.

- It can make it easier if you need to shut down. If you must unwind your business, and heaven forbid consider bankruptcy, then having separated your purchases onto separate cards will make it easier to identify which ones were for business purposes and which ones weren't.

Of course, you have a choice of whether to use a business or a personal credit card for the purchases you make for your business. While, technically, you aren't supposed to use a personal credit card for your business, it's not that hard to do. It's not like your card issuer is looking over your shoulder and questioning whether that paper you purchased is really for your kid's school supplies instead of for your business. (They earn their percentage in either case.)

In the past, the decision between using a small business card and a personal one was pretty easy. But it's become more complicated thanks to the Credit CARD Act. That legislation, which was passed in 2009, gave consumers significant protections when it comes to their credit cards. It stopped the practices for example of raising interest rates on outstanding credit card balances at any time for any reason, and restricted penalty fees, among other things.

This law, however, specifically excludes business credit cards. So that means that a card issuer can still raise interest rates on business or corporate credit cards at any time, or set cutoff times for a payment to be received in the middle of the day, instead of by 5 PM as required by the CARD Act, for example. And those are just a couple of examples of the protections that don't automatically come with business credit cards.

Fortunately, some card issuers have extended some of the protections the CARD Act offers to their small business cards. If this is important to you, then look for a card that offers these protections.

Summary of Protections Under the Credit CARD Act

Here are some of the consumer protections offered under the federal CARD Act. Again, these apply to personal—not small business—credit cards, though, as mentioned, some issuers include these on their business cards.

Before changing your interest rate, increasing fees, or making other significant changes to the terms of your credit card, your card issuer must send you 45 days advance written notice. You then have the option to "opt out" of the change in terms and pay back the balance at the previous terms. (You may have to close your account.)

Your issuer can't raise your rate the first year unless you are 60 days late with a payment, your card has a variable rate tied to an index that changes, or an introductory rate expires.

No "floating" due dates are allowed. Your due date must be the same date each month and the cut-off time for receiving payments can't be earlier than 5 pm. If your due date falls on a weekend or holiday when your issuer doesn't accept payments, you can make your payment the following business day without penalty.

If you pay more than the minimum payment due, your card issuer must apply the amount over the minimum toward the portion of the balance with the highest interest rate, not the lowest rate as they did before this law went into place.

Late fees are capped at a "reasonable amount" (generally $25) and card issuers can't charge an over-limit fee unless the consumer has "opted in" to allow their card to go over the limit.

If small business or corporate cards don't offer those protections, then why would you, as a business owner, even consider one? One good reason is to help protect your personal credit. Balances on your personal cards almost always show up on your credit reports, but balances on business cards aren't typically reported to the personal credit reporting agencies. If your business relies heavily on credit cards for financing, it's helpful to keep that information off your personal credit reports so that your credit scores don't drop due to the maxxed out credit card. A warning: Do not assume that if one of these accounts does not currently appear on your credit reports that it will never show up there. Almost all small business cards will require a personal guarantee and will report payment history to the guarantor's personal credit if the account goes into default. Out of the top ten issuers of these cards, only one does not report *any* payment information to the owner's personal credit reports.

In addition, around the time the Credit CARD Act became law, one of the major issuers of small business cards decided to start reporting *all* of the activity of their small business cards on the owners' personal credit reports. Some business owners saw their credit scores plummet due to the debt they were carrying on one of these cards. Because their credit scores dropped, they were having a hard time getting a different card to use to transfer the balance. It was truly a Catch-22.

Can one of these cards help you build business credit? It depends. Most of them do report payment history to at least one of the major corporate credit reporting agencies. However, unlike personal credit cards which almost always show up on all three of your major credit reports (at Equifax, Experian, and TransUnion), these cards may not report to all of the major agencies we will describe later.

If you are confident in your ability to manage one of these accounts successfully, then hold on to those offers you receive and spend a little time comparing them. You can also get more information on credit card offers in our Resource Section. You can also use a website like Credit.com which compares offers for you. Just don't apply for multiple cards at once. Each issuer will almost always run a credit check on your personal credit, and that will appear on your credit report as an inquiry. Recent inquiries can lower your credit score slightly, so only apply for one card at a time and make sure it's one you really want.

As long as you have decent personal credit scores, it's usually not that hard to get one of these cards, even if your business is relatively new. You may have to settle for a smaller credit line or you may have to get a charge card that requires you to pay your balances in full each month, but most people will be able to qualify for one. When you do, you may find yourself in a good position to earn lucrative rewards for your business spending. Those may include airline miles or points toward travel or merchandise. The rewards on business cards are similar to those for premium personal credit cards. And as long as you pay in full each month to avoid interest, one of these cards can be an excellent deal.

- Retail and gas cards are the easiest for businesses to get without a personal guarantee.
- Major business credit cards (American Express, Discover, MasterCard, Visa) are more widely accepted, but usually require personal guarantees unless your business is well-established.

- Again, do not fill out multiple card applications at once. Doing so can create multiple inquiries on your credit file, and a result in denial.
- After you have had a business card for at least six months and have paid it on time, you may want to request a credit line increase.

We will explore the additional steps for building business credit in Chapter 13. For now, let's get a business loan…

Chapter 3

Small Business Loans

Starting a business can be exhilarating; a leap of faith into the unknown, if you will. Those words also describe what Aaron and Kathy Corr's customers often experience when they visit TreeUmph!, a fourteen-acre elevated obstacle course in the tree-tops for adults and kids ages 7 and older. At TreeUmph!, the adventure includes wobbly bridges, tightropes, hanging nets, swinging ropes and, of course, ziplines. It opened in January, 2013 in Bradenton, Florida and the response from the community has been enthusiastic.

But getting the business off the ground proved to be more difficult than the Corrs expected. Like many entrepreneurs, they tapped everything they could to get it started, including personal savings, personal loans, and funds from friends and family. "We're fortunate to have a good strong team and good capitalization," says Aaron. In fact, they thought they were good to go, but discovered that there were a lot of state, and municipal, and regulatory requirements that required additional funds.

So they went looking for a small business loan. "We were very confident we could find the money we needed because we knew we had a good idea, a good business plan, and we were well-capitalized," Aaron says. "But we had a bit of a rude awakening when we started going to banks looking for the additional funding we needed. We literally were refused at the door at the banks that we went to because they would not deal with startup businesses."

Finally they approached a community bank that was willing to listen to their plans.

Shaun Merriman, president and CEO of Gateway Bank, says that two things set Aaron and his wife Kathy apart: their passion and their planning. "I could tell that this was something that they'd been working on a long time. It was one of the best designed business plans that I have ever seen in 28 years. Their plan was one of the most comprehensive, well-organized, and well thought through." As a result, Gateway Bank was able to make the loan, and the Corr's were able to launch a business that's been garnering rave reviews.

When it comes to borrowing from a bank, who knows better than a banker? For this section, Tom Trafficante, the Executive Vice President and Chief Credit Officer at Heritage Bank of Nevada, provides his thoughts.

Before You Apply for Small Business Loan

You know the saying, "You only get one chance to make a first impression?" That's true in many aspects of business, including when you apply for a small business loan. Before making a formal application to a bank for a small business loan, be sure to research banks and other lending institutions which are actively making small business loans in your community and arrange a meeting with at least two of these lenders.

There are multiple government and non-profit agencies in most communities to assist small businesses with planning and counseling, including assistance in preparing a business loan application. These include the U.S. Small Business Administration (SBA), Small Business Development Center, SCORE, Chamber of Commerce and Economic Development Agencies. By first contacting one of these agencies, you will be able to determine which banks are more aggressively seeking loans and obtain a referral to meet with them. You should also contact your own accountant, attorney, insurance broker or business associate for a similar reference.

Once your list of banks is narrowed down to two or three, set up a meeting with each bank to discuss your individual situation with them. You should take the opportunity to better understand the bank's procedures for processing and approving the type and size loan you are looking for.

Factors Used by Banks to Evaluate Business Loans

The application process

The process used by a bank to evaluate small business loans varies considerably for each institution and is based on several factors. The size and complexity of loan request determines the depth and nature of the underwriting process. For smaller business loan requests (typically loan requests less than $100,000), most banks use a more streamlined approval process or automated underwriting process. Some banks utilize automated credit scoring systems for loan requests as high as $250,000.

Credit scoring models are heavily reliant on the strength of the credit reports of both the business and the principal owners of the business who will be required to guarantee the loan. In addition to information obtained from credit reporting agencies, the automated system will use income and asset information from the applicant's tax returns and from the application to underwrite the loan for sufficient cash flow and liquid assets.

Most banks will require that they be able to review three years of operating history for the business and three years' financial information from any principal owner with 20% or more ownership interest in order to obtain a commercial loan. Generally, for a business with less than two years of operating history, the business will be considered a "start-up" and generally will not qualify for a conventional loan with a bank. Only in cases where the principal owners have sources of income and strong cash balances to support the loan repayment without the business income, would they be considered by a bank for a start-up business loan. Some banks will consider a loan to a start-up business with an SBA guarantee, but even with the SBA guarantee (discussed in Chapter 4) most banks will not consider a start-up business for financing. If the loan request is declined by the automated system or when the loan request exceeds the threshold amount of $100,000, then the loan is processed with great detail and scrutiny.

What is required to apply for a small business loan

Typically, a small business loan request will require the following information:

- The business tax returns for the most recent three year period
- The personal tax returns of the all principal owners for the most recent three year period
- The fiscal year end business financial statements for the most recent three year period
- Interim financial statement (since the most recent fiscal year end)
- Personal financial statement of the principal owners
- Liquid asset verification and debt schedules for both the business and the principal owner

- Other pertinent information about the company and its principal owners
- A current year budget or projection may be requested

Once this information is received by the bank, a credit analyst will create a financial spreadsheet which displays the historical financial information in various formats, calculates numerous ratios and trends, and then compares the information to other companies of similar size in the same industry. You should request a copy of these spreadsheets whether your loan is approved or not, as there is often valuable information for your own consideration.

The financial spreadsheets are then sent to a loan officer for review and underwriting. If the loan officer determines that the request is eligible for consideration, the officer will compile a credit memorandum which summarizes the loan request, the financial condition of the applicant, variances from lending policy and risks associated with the request. The credit memorandum could be a few pages or longer than 100 pages, depending upon the size, nature and complexity of the loan.

Loan officers may have some direct authority to make a loan, but generally loan approval will require the signature of a credit administrator. If the credit request is larger, typically over $1 million or more, the loan request will need to be approved by a loan committee. In most cases, a loan which is approved by the loan officer and the credit administrator will rarely be declined by a loan committee.

Obtaining Loan Approval

The commercial loan underwriting process can be very complex and is beyond the scope of this book to fully describe. However, there are some basic financial data and ratios that are the key to obtain loan approval. The first is the amount and stability of historical and projected cash flow of the business. The second is the amount of debt and equity and available collateral for the loan. And lastly is the liquidity and financial strength of the principal owners of the business who guarantee the loan.

Loans are expected to be repaid from future excess cash flow, and thus the biggest issue for a loan officer to consider is if the cash flow is adequate to repay the loan. It is important to distinguish between net income and cash flow. A simplified approach, called Traditional Cash Flow method, will average the company's prior three years of net earnings (net income), plus interest, plus other non-cash expenses like depreciation and amortization (this number is referred to as EBITDA). Using the EBITDA, the loan officer will calculate the current principal and interest payments of the existing debt, plus the principal and interest on the requested debt (this number is referred to as Debt Service). The loan officer calculates a debt service coverage ratio (DSCR) by taking EBITDA divided by Debt Service. This ratio should exceed 1.20. In other words, the company should show historically that it has 20% extra cash flow above the proposed loan's payments.

Aside from the traditional historical cash flow, the loan officer will consider the trend of the sales and expenses and look for improving or declining cash flow. He will also review the balance sheet for other sources and uses of cash. Other uses of cash include such items as capital expenditures, and growth of accounts receivable and inventory relative to trade payables and other financing.

The second significant loan underwriting concern is the amount of debt and equity. The loan officer will calculate a debt to equity ratio by looking at the company's total debt divided by the amount of equity. The total debt should be less than 4 times the equity. In other words, the company should have at least 20% equity. Equity provides a cushion above the debt which allows the company to be sold or liquidated and still be able to repay the loan.

The company's assets are usually pledged as collateral for the loan. Collateral is a specific asset (or assets) which is pledged to the bank to secure repayment of the debt. For financially strong companies and guarantors, banks will make unsecured loans. However, most small business loans are secured by the company's assets, such as its inventory, receivables and other fixed assets. In the event of default, the bank will have the right to repossess and sell the assets or collect the receivables to repay the loan.

The final consideration is the principal owner's financial strength. In almost all cases, small business loans made by financial institutions will require the personal guarantee of any principal owner with 20% or more ownership of the company. If the business defaults on the loan, the bank will have the right to pursue the owner of the company. Loan approval considers the liquid assets, personal cash flow and overall net worth of the principal owner, especially if the primary cash flow and collateral offered by the business are not sufficient. The bank may ask that the principal owner pledge additional collateral to support the loan if the company's assets are not adequate collateral for the loan

What If The Loan Is Declined?

If your loan request is declined, you are entitled to be told specifically why you have been declined. The best strategy is to meet face-to-face with the loan officer and discuss the specific reasons for the decline. You should inquire about what changes or benchmark ratios need to be improved to obtain a loan.

If the loan officer is not an SBA loan specialist or the bank is not an active SBA lender, you should meet with the SBA officer or locate the most active SBA lender in the community. The SBA guarantees a significant portion of the loan principal (up to 90%) and many banks and other non-bank financial institutions will make loans declined by banks. You should also go back to some of the resources mentioned in this book and begin searching for alternative lending sources. There are many sources of financing available and strategies to become "bankable" if you search for them.

Thank you, Tom, for your valuable insights.

We will discuss SBA loans in the next chapter. But first, it is appropriate to provide several more tips for dealing with banks, or any lender for that matter.

Where Do I Stand?

If the numbers and formulas we've been describing in this chapter make your head spin or your eyes cross, you may check out a couple of simple tools that can help you (and lenders) handle your businesses' overall financial health.

Sageworks is an internet company that develops products that can be used by small businesses, accountants and other financial advisors, as well as lenders, to evaluate the financial health of a business. According to Sageworks, there are five main financial statement ratios that creditors frequently use to evaluate the financial performance of a private company. They are:

- Cash to Assets
- EBITDA to Assets

- Debt Service Coverage Ratio
- Liabilities to Assets
- Net Income to Sales

With the Sagework platform, eight to ten pieces of information can be entered to produce a report that will help evaluate the businesses' financial statements and analyze what they are doing well, as well as what areas may need improvement.

"Some businesses will run these reports to see where they stand before they talk to a banker. It's a quick proxy for what will I hear from my bank?," says analyst Libby Bierman. But a business owner can also use it, "for leverage or to negotiate for better payment terms," she says, if the financial health of the business is strong. For more information, including free white-papers on business credit topics, visit our Resource Section.

Dress for Success

It should almost go without saying that when you meet with a banker or other lender you should dress appropriately. We've added the word 'almost' to that last sentence in recognition of how informally people conduct themselves now. Most of you know how to dress. But clearly—the evidence is all around us—some people don't. So while we don't want to come across as a nag or a scold, if your idea of formal is a T-shirt without holes in it, we have some work to do. The point of this book is to get your business financed. You've got to use every strategy and tactic to get it done. Show the lender some respect by dressing appropriately. (For an entertaining and interesting perspective on this topic, read Crazy Egg founder Neil Patel's post, "How Spending $162,301.42 on Clothes Made Me $692,500" on his website, Quicksprout.com.)

Avoid High Salaries and Entertainment Expenses

Lenders want their money to be applied to the business. They don't want that money going to your salary and your enjoyment. They want you committed to the business by taking a low salary at the start and foregoing the perks of larger businesses.

A Winning Business Plan

There is considerable debate about whether a business plan is a necessity. Some entrepreneurs say they either never created a business plan, or if they did, never used it. And it's true that in certain circles (especially those trying to raise money in Silicon Valley) a "pitch deck" is considered more appropriate than a formal business plan. (We will discuss the pitch deck in more detail in Chapter 14.)

But banks and other financial institutions tend to be traditionalists, and they often want to see a well thought out and well drafted business plan. (In certain countries, such as Germany and Peru, a business plan is an absolute necessity.) Not only does a business plan serve as a road map for where you are headed but for lenders it is the starting point of the journey. It also forces you to ask hard questions about your business and where you see it headed. Those are the same questions that a bank or other lender will ask. The proper drafting of a business plan is a book unto itself. Please consider reading Garrett Sutton's *Writing Winning Business Plans*.

Even the SBA says a business plan is "an essential roadmap for business success." SBA loans are up next...

Chapter 4

SBA Loans

For years, Leslie had dreamed of opening her own one-stop event shop that combined her exceptional baking skills, her background in design, and her experience as a florist. Having worked part-time for years for a well-established florist in Austin, Texas, Leslie had aspirations of taking over the shop when the owners retired, which they'd announced would be soon.

Leslie, was anxious to get started. But then, the flower shop owners told her that they had decided not to retire after all. It was time for Leslie to take matters into her own hands.

The business plan she'd been tinkering with for years became her sole focus. Despite being in the midst of the worst economic downturn since The Great Depression, Leslie worked feverishly with her local Small Business Development Center to formulate a comprehensive, realistic, thorough business plan for the flower shop.

"The flower shop seemed like the hardest hurdle," Leslie says. "Getting a retail base and a clientele so that it can sustain itself seemed like the best way to start, and then down the road I could expand to include the culinary aspect. You have your first-year goals, then your five-year, your ten-year ... but this was the best place to start."

That same month, Leslie's counselor at the Small Business Development Center advised her to apply for an SBA-backed loan, as part of a program that was set to expire at the end of April. The center had worked with a bank in Florida in the past, and had been very helpful with their advisees; Leslie's plan had a shot, and it was worth applying.

Leslie filled out the 7-page application, and submitted her business plan, along with a lot of other documentation, to the bank, and by the end of March, she learned that she'd been approved for a $50,000, SBA-backed Community Express Loan, as part of the bank's Express Capital Loan program.

Leslie still needed to come up with the 10 percent down payment on her downtown Austin location—the loan wouldn't cover this. Fortunately, Leslie had also entered a business plan competition, and she learned in April that her plan had taken third prize. Her winnings enabled her to make the down payment.

Leslie opened her shop in the summer, and began making payments to the bank just one month after receiving her disbursement. "The loan was my working capital. I was able to get the bills paid and buy some inventory," she says, explaining that she had made a practice of collecting deep-discounted inventory over the years, which really kept her initial costs down. "Being able to have extra capital in the first six months, when I was still building a client base, was really important."

Within her first nine months, her business had hired three part-timers, took on an intern/business assistant, been ranked by Austin's local alternative weekly paper among the top three florists in town on its "Best of Austin" list, and broke even financially. "I'm still not taking a salary yet," Leslie says a year and a half after opening her doors, "but the business is now holding its own. We did $250,000 in our first year."

Leslie says that although her SBA-backed loan was relatively small in comparison to some other business loans out there, without it her dream might not have come true—at least, not so quickly.

Leslie is among a growing number of Americans who have been able to start or grow their businesses thanks to the Small Business Administration, which guarantees privately funded loans through several loan programs that target a variety of businesses. The SBA now facilitates the lending of tens of billions of dollars every year. And for many businesses, these loans mean the difference between being in business and closing their doors (or never opening them in the first place).

The SBA's Loan Programs

Businesses usually seek capital for one of two reasons: 1) They're in survival mode, trying to start up or simply stay in business, or 2) They're looking to expand.

Businesses in survival mode are looking for subsistence funding just to stay alive. In the case of start-ups, they need money to secure locations, purchase materials and inventory, develop marketing materials, and pay the bills so they can keep their lights on. For other businesses that may have already been in existence, they're in survival mode because of any number of factors—an economic downturn, construction blocking their entrance, or the emergence of a new competitor, for example.

On the other hand, expansion-mode businesses have a track record of success. They're profitable and need to grow to increase profits and meet consumer demand. Banks like expansion-mode businesses.

But it's often survival-mode businesses, particularly in a tough economic times, that are seeking loans. Perhaps they've exhausted all their families' and friends' resources, have maxed out their credit cards, or simply can't afford to compete without an injection of funds.

Meanwhile, most commercial lending banks see survival-mode businesses as a great risk; they often prefer lending to businesses that are expanding, who can prove their accomplishments and have considerable assets that ensure they can pay back their loans. And this simply isn't possible for many small businesses. Here's where the SBA steps in.

First, it's important to note that the SBA itself actually doesn't do any lending. Rather, it sets guidelines for loans made by traditional lenders that it partners with, then acts as a guarantor for those loans made to business owners who might have trouble qualifying for traditional bank loans. The guaranty provided by the SBA on a large percentage of the loan ensures the bank that the majority of the loan will be paid back.

To get an SBA loan, a business owner goes to one of the SBA's partner banks or lending institutions and applies for the loan directly through this lender. If approved, the loan is eligible for an SBA guaranty, which is a percentage that represents the portion of the loan that the SBA will repay the bank if the business owner defaults on the loan.

The SBA guaranty, at the time of this writing, covers up to 85 percent of the loan amount, which is a considerably lower-risk proposition for banks than loaning to unproven businesses.

The Guaranteed Loan Programs offered by the SBA vary depending on your needs and the size of your business. One of the loan programs is:

Basic 7(a) Loan Program

The 7(a) loan, according to the SBA's website, provides eligible borrowers with up to $5 million in capital for "starting, acquiring and expanding a small business. This type of loan is the most basic and the most used within SBA's business loan programs." All owners of a business with at least a 20 percent stake in ownership must personally guarantee the loan.

A 7(a) loan may be used to:

- Purchase land or buildings, including conversion of existing facilities or new construction

- Purchase equipment, supplies, furniture, and materials

- Maintain short- and long-term working capital for such things as payments on accounts receivable, seasonal financing, contract performance, construction financing, or export production

- Refinance certain business debt with unreasonable terms or conditions

- Purchase an existing business

Borrowers may not use a 7(a) loan to effect a change of ownership or practice that would not benefit the business, pay delinquent taxes or other funds held in trust or escrow, refinance existing debt that would create a loss for the lender, or for any business purpose that the lender may find to be unsound.

The eligibility criteria for 7(a) loans are the broadest of all the SBA's guarantee programs. This program targets small businesses, which the SBA defines as "one that is independently owned and operated, is organized for profit, and is not dominant in its field." In general, depending on the business type the business' annual receipts may have a cap at between $2.5 to $21.5 million. And despite the loan being designed to help start-up businesses, most lenders won't make this loan to businesses that don't have two or three years' worth of financial statements and an owner with equity in the business.

Under the umbrella of the 7(a) program are some specialty loan programs:

SBAExpress: Aimed at expediting the loan application process and getting loans of up to $350,000 quickly into entrepreneurs' hands, this program targets business owners with a good borrowing track record. It involves a speedy response time of 36 hours and, often, a low interest rate. The downside of this, however, is that the expedited processing time comes with greater risk and, therefore, a lower guarantee of just 50 percent.

Small Loan Advantage: The Advantage programs also involve streamlined application processes. Guaranteeing 85 percent of loans up to $250,000 and 75 percent for amounts greater, the SBA offers this loan to larger businesses looking to borrow small amounts, which benefits businesses in underserved areas. The application for this loan is only two pages, and most of them can be approved in minutes with electronic submission.

Community Advantage: This is another Advantage program that targets underserved communities. This three-year pilot program begun in January 2015 is designed to increase the number of lenders that can make SBA 7(a) loans to distressed and underserved communities. With a maximum loan size of $250,000, this loan features streamlined paperwork, a two-page application, and an approval process of ten days or less. The program targets communities, such as minorities, women, veterans, and businesses in rural or low-income areas. Borrowers are encouraged, as part of the application process, to work with advisors on developing business plans.

CDC/504 Loan Program:

The SBA's website says that as of January 2015, this loan program had provided $50 billion in loans and created more than two million jobs. It's designed for small business owners looking to purchase assets or finance real estate for expansion. This program may be particularly important for businesses, for example, in which heavy machinery and rapidly advancing technology play a key role; without an injection of loan monies for such acquisitions, a business may simply be unable to compete in its field.

These loans are provided through Certified Development Companies, or CDCs, which are nonprofit corporations that promote community economic development in specific geographic areas across the country. (CDCs may be accessed through your local SBA office. You'll find a list of SBA offices at http://www.sba.gov/about-offices-list/2.)

In a 504 loan, the SBA guarantees a CDC-provided loan of up to 40 percent of the total project cost; a participating lender kicks in 50 percent, and the borrower covers the last 10 percent. The 504 loan comes with long amortization periods, fixed interest rates, and no balloon payments. There is no maximum project size, but the maximum loan amount is $5 million.

Here is how it benefits the community and the economy to make these loans available: The program stipulates that unless your business meets specific community development standards for underserved communities as set forth by the CDC, it must either create or retain a job for each $65,000 guaranteed by the SBA (or $100,000 for small manufacturers.)

A 504 loan may be used to:
- Purchase or improve existing buildings
- Make improvements to the land

- Modernize, upgrade, retrofit, or convert existing facilities
- Purchase new machinery

A 504 loan is, of course, not accessible for start-ups. It may not be used for working capital, inventory, to refinance such debt, or to consolidate or pay off debt.

Eligible businesses must be for-profit, non-speculative entities and must be considered a small-business concern, in accordance with the SBA's definition.

Microloan Program

As their name implies, microloans are small, short-term loans offered through microlenders, which are nonprofit economic development organizations approved by the SBA. They are usually offered to neighborhood, mom-and-pop-type businesses, or those small businesses that have credit challenges, because many people who can't qualify for traditional bank loans may qualify for microloans.

You'll find a list of microlenders near you on the SBA.gov website, and we will talk more about microloans in the next chapter.

Special Interest Loans:

Through the SBA's loan program are several specialized loans designed for very particular types of businesses.

Special Purpose: These three 7(a) loans include the *Community Adjustment and Investment Program (CAIP)* intended to assist small businesses that have been negatively affected by NAFTA; the *CAPLines Program*, for businesses needing assistance with short-term or cyclical working capital needs (for instance, hiring additional workers for the holiday season); and *Pollution Control* loans, which provide aid to businesses looking to reduce their environmental footprint. (Know that some loans are not always available due to a lack of appropriations.)

Export Loan Programs: According to the SBA website, about 70 percent of all U.S. exporters are businesses with 20 or fewer employees. This loan program was designed by the SBA specifically to help these businesses develop or enhance their export activities. Within this category are several programs, including an *Export Express Program*, which offers expedited processing of loans up to $500,000; an *Export Working Capital Program (EWCP)*, in which the SBA guarantees up to 90 percent of loans up to $5 million as credit enhancements, to assist the working capital needs of businesses involved in exporting (a category often dismissed by traditional lenders); and the *International Trade Loan Program*, which is intended to help businesses finance the purchase of fixed assets to develop or continue exporting activities.

Rural Lender Advantage: The Small/Rural Lender Advantage program is intended to assist small community or rural-based lenders with processing business loans of $350,000 or less. It includes a two-page application, an 80 percent loan guarantee, expedited processing, fax and online application submissions, and simplified eligibility requirements. Under this heading is the *B&I Guaranteed Loan Program*, a loan for small businesses in rural communities that is maintained by the U.S. Department of Agriculture, for the purposes of assisting businesses with working capital, machinery and equipment purchases, buildings and real estate, and certain types of debt refinancing.

Disaster Loans: The SBA offers several long-term, low-interest loans for businesses and individuals negatively affected by natural disasters. See SBA.gov for a complete list of disaster loan programs and eligibility requirements.

Veteran and Military Community Loans: Intended for businesses and individuals affected by military service, the *Military Reservist Economic Injury Disaster Loan*, is for small businesses that are unable to meet their necessary expenses as a direct result of essential employees being called up from reserves to active duty.

Other Financial Assistance:

For those unable or unwilling to take out loans, there may be other sources of financial assistance, including government and research grants and venture capital. While these are not provided or backed by the SBA, its website, SBA.gov, provides information, listings, and tools for finding this assistance.

How to Apply for an SBA Loan

In recent years the SBA has provided record numbers of loans to small business owners. This increase may have been driven in part by the SBA's effort to streamline the application process and get more loan money into the hands of business owners.

Nonetheless, it is lenders, and not the SBA, that provide the applications, so you must contact a participating SBA lender directly to apply.

Each lender has its own specific requirements. In general, your application will usually require you to provide details about who you are, including your professional and financial history, as well as the finances of all principals in the business. You'll need to describe your business, your competitors, your challenges, your plans for borrowed funds, your plans for loan repayment, your projections for the near future of the business, and your collateral.

You may also be asked by your lender to provide a lease, franchise agreement, purchase agreement, articles of incorporation, plans/specifications, copies of licenses, letters of reference or intent, contracts, or partnership agreements.

The SBA Loan Application Checklist is an 11-item list of forms and documents you'll need to provide to your lender as part of the process:

1. **Your SBA loan application (SBA Form 4)** — may be downloaded from SBA.gov

2. **Personal background and financial statement** — SBA Form 912 (Statement of Personal History) and SBA Form 413 (Personal Financial Statement)

3. **Business financial statements** — a current profit-and-loss (P&L) sheet and a detailed, one-year projection of income and finances, attached to an explanation about how you intend to meet this projection

4. **Ownership and affiliations** — names and contact information for anyone holding a controlling interest in the business, subsidiaries, or affiliates

5. **Business certificate/license** — original business license or certificate to do business

6. **Loan application history** — records of previously applied-for loans

7. **Income tax returns** — personal and business for all principals for the last three years

8. **Resumes**—for each principal or member of the management team

9. **Business overview and history**—a brief history of your business and its challenges, including an explanation of why you need the loan

10. **Business lease**—either a lease or a note detailing the terms of the lease from a landlord

11. **Items for purchasing an existing business**—if your loan would be for the purchase of an existing business, you'll need a current balance sheet and P&L of business to be purchased, its previous two years of income tax statements, a proposed Bill of Sale, and the asking price (with details about schedule of inventory, machinery, furniture, etc.)

To be sure, applying for an SBA-backed loan can be a lengthy, sometimes frustrating process. It certainly points to the need to have a solid business plan and detailed financial records.

And because lenders set their own requirements (within the context of SBA guidelines, of course), this also means it may make sense for you to work with a company that can help you find the right SBA lending partner.

The Downside of SBA Loans

An SBA loan that helps your business grow is terrific, but if you run into tough times, one of these loans can turn into a nightmare. That's because the same federal guarantee and collateral requirements that make these loans work can work *against* the borrower.

SBA loans almost always require a personal guarantee from the principals of the business. And for many loans, the borrower must pledge all available capital. That means, for example, if you have equity in your home you will likely have to pledge that collateral for the loan.

Though the federal government guarantees most of the loan, that guarantee is designed to protect the lender—not the borrower. When a borrower defaults, the government doesn't just hand the lender a check and walk away. Instead, there will be a serious effort to collect as much as possible. Collection efforts are almost always handled by the lenders themselves and may include:

1. Trying to collect from the owner of the business, who in most cases provided a personal guarantee. If necessary, they may sue the business and/or person(s) who agreed to be personally liable for the debt and get a judgment, which opens up new avenues for collection.

2. Foreclosing upon or repossessing any collateral pledged for the loan, including personal assets (a home, for example) and/or business assets (equipment, inventory, etc.).

If you fall behind on an SBA loan, reach out for help. You may be able to settle the debt for less than you owe, or renegotiate the terms while your business gets back on its feet. Your attorney, CPA or a firm that helps business owners in distress may be able to assist if you can't do this on your own.

Another option may be bankruptcy. While it may not be ideal, it may give you the fresh start you need to regroup and try again.

Keep in mind that if you default on an SBA loan you personally guaranteed you may receive a 1099-C reporting the cancelled debts as "income," which could create a whole new set of problems. Since forgiveness of debt is income you now owe the IRS on that "income." Be sure to discuss this issue with your accountant or CPA if you fall behind on your loan. Maybe a smaller loan is best for you...

Chapter 5

Think Small: Microloans, CDFI's and Credit Unions

Carlos was recovering from spinal surgery. When it became clear that he couldn't return to being a painting contractor, he needed to find another career. After reminiscing about food trucks at a party, Carlos and his wife Maria drew up plans for a 'tricked out' truck with pin striping and a rockin' stereo system. They took their plan to a regular bank, but didn't get very far. In fact, the bank didn't get it and told Carlos and Maria that they were too much of a risk.

They were referred to a non-bank micro-lender by a friend. When Maria and Carlos presented their idea to the micro lender they got it and loaned the couple $35,000. "They didn't laugh," said Maria. "They went all the way with us which was so cool. During the first year, we called our rep. 'We are struggling, and we don't know what to do' and they were always supportive. We wouldn't still be here without our lender in that first year."

Carlos and Maria specialize in Tex/Mex food and they cater corporate events and street festivals. They became so successful that they went to CDC Small Business Finance for a bigger loan to pay off the first loan and buy another truck. They now have three trucks and are looking at a fourth, have two employees besides themselves and hire lots of independent contractors.

For many banks, especially regional or national ones, a very small loan to a very small business simply isn't profitable. However, one of these loans—often dubbed "microloans"—can make or break a new venture. That's where microlending organizations come in.

Usually, things that would be problematic in traditional loans—a bad credit history or lack of collateral, for example—aren't necessarily strikes with microlenders, who not only provide loans of up to $50,000 but will also provide training and mentoring to borrowers. If you want microloan funds, you must be prepared to fulfill their training and planning requirements before they'll even consider your application.

Microloan program loans are offered to small business concerns and certain not-for-profit childcare centers. Designed for survival-mode businesses, microloans aren't intended for paying existing debts or purchasing real estate. They may be used for the following:

- Working capital
- Purchase of inventory and supplies
- Purchase of furniture and fixtures
- Purchase of machinery and equipment

Because of the terms and amounts of microloans, SBA microloans come with a shorter term and higher interest rates. The maximum length is six years, and rates range from 8–13 percent.

Microlending at Work

CAMEO, the California Association for Micro Enterprise Opportunity, demonstrates the power of microlending. According to Claudia Viek, their CEO, CAMEO has been creating jobs since its inception in 1993 by helping people to be their own boss or, in other words, to create their own job. Their mission is to grow a healthy, vibrant, thriving environment for all entrepreneurs and start-up businesses by advancing the work of their statewide member network.

Cameo's 85 member organizations provide the entire spectrum of entrepreneurs with small and micro-business financing, technical assistance and business management training. In 2013, CAMEO members served 15,000 very small businesses that supported or created thousands of new jobs in California and generated over a billion dollars in economic activity. This success is possible because members offer a rich continuum of business services. Research in this field shows that businesses that receive assistance have an 80% success rate as compared with the 50% to 80% mortality rate for small businesses overall.

In other words, they don't just make loans. They help businesses succeed.

As California's statewide Micro Enterprise association, CAMEO expands resources and builds the capacity of member organizations. For example, CAMEO works with corporations and government to leverage new capital and grants. Wells Fargo, Chase Bank and even Chevron have made significant new investments and grants to microlenders. However, achieving scale in microlending has significant barriers. Operating costs are high due to a small capital base and the extra expense of providing technical and business assistance. CAMEO has put in place innovative online platforms to scale up microlending in California. Because lending requires volume the platforms reduce operating costs and facilitate small business capital.

Not every state has a microlending organization like CAMEO. For more information on them visit www.microbiz. org. But there are micro lenders out there, as we will discuss.

The Landscape of Microlending

A recent opinion poll by Small Business Majority, Main Street Alliance and the American Sustainable Business Council found that "90 percent of small business owners believe the availability of credit is a problem, and three in five say it is harder to get a loan now than it was four years ago." The larger banks have pulled back on loans under $250,000. The problem is the small loans cost about the same in transaction costs as a $1 million loan. So if traditional banks aren't lending where can small businesses find funding to run their businesses and help with cash flow?

The answer is to look for alternative lending sources, such as microlenders and community development financial institutions (CDFIs), including community development credit unions.

Microlenders/CDFIs often make loans under $50,000. These loans include those financed by the Small Business Administration Micro Loan Fund, USDA Rural Development loans and community development loans by local governments, banks and donors. Microlenders place more emphasis on cash flow than collateral, and give more weight to the character of the borrower.

Community Development Financial Institutions

If you've been in a Starbucks in recent years, you may have seen red, white and blue bracelets offered for a donation of $5 or more to the Jobs for USA campaign. Starbucks joined forces with Opportunity Finance Network, a network of Community Development Financial Institutions (CDFIs), to help raise money for loans to small businesses and seeded this campaign with a $5 million donation.

If you donated to the campaign, as the authors of this book did, you may not have entirely understood what you were supporting. In fact, it's possible that this campaign could become a source of funding for your business, or that of someone in your community.

CDFIs include non-profit loan funds, credit unions, banks and venture funds that focus on making loans to underserved communities. In addition to making personal loans, they are often a crucial source of funding for small businesses that have been turned down for loans from traditional sources. CDFIs may provide funding for small businesses, microenterprises, nonprofit organizations, commercial real estate, and affordable housing.

The group that Starbucks partnered with, Opportunity Finance Network, has originated more than $30 billion in funding in urban, rural and Native communities. In particular, CDFIs often focus on low-income and/or minority communities, though applicants shouldn't be discouraged from reaching out to one if they are having trouble getting funding and don't meet any of those criteria.

If you apply for a loan through a CDFI, you should expect that the lender will run a personal credit check on you, the owner. It's likely that your credit score will be considered in the application process; but it's usually only one part of the decision and most CDFIs will tell you that even with past credit problems you may still be eligible for loans. In addition, CDFIs may be able to consider non-traditional credit references, such as rent or utility payments, for example.

Typically, these loans require collateral and/or personal guarantees as well.

CDFI's offer loans of varying sizes including microloans as well as some that go as high as $250,000. Many CDFIs provide small-business coaching and other professional resources, such as legal, accounting, and marketing assistance, to grow their borrowers' small businesses. CDFIs usually:

- have more flexibility with their collateral and credit requirements (they accept good, but not perfect credit)
- are willing to consider explanations for lower credit score (such as loss of home equity, late pays, illness)
- consider the character of the borrower
- offer reasonable loan terms and try to make sure the borrower thoroughly understands them

However, businesses still need to show the ability to pay back the loan through positive cash flows and have a marketing plan to guide growth. The loan criteria is often listed on the lender's website and vary in terms of a business location, loan size, interest rates, risk, or borrower income.

CDFI's want to "make loans that change lives," says Mark Pinskey, President and CEO of Opportunity Finance Network.

Finding Microlenders

The first real step is to research alternative lenders in your area or those that lend online without regard to geographical location. Look for an established government agency or nonprofit, such as Community Development Financial Institutions and credit unions. Some city and county governments run microloan programs. Talk with your local economic development or business development agency. Other good sources for loans referrals are Small Business Development Centers and micro enterprise development organizations. While most of them don't lend money, they are often connected to the capital resources in their communities. (See lending and business resources in the Resource Section.) Opportunity Finance Network also maintains a free locator service for member programs on its website.

The second step to finding a small or micro-business loan is to make sure that you are loan-ready, i.e. that you meet the criteria. That means that you have satisfactory answers to the following:

- What is the purpose of the loan?
- How the loan will be repaid?
- What is Plan B for repayment?
- Do you have a business plan?
- Do you have financial statements? (Cash flow and P & Ls)
- What is your collateral?

If you don't meet the criteria, then seek out help from a local entrepreneurial training provider. Not only will they help a business obtain a loan, but they will help locally grown small and micro-businesses become successful.

Finally, be prepared to give the lender what they ask for. Entrepreneurial training organizations often can help you with loan packaging, such as putting your documents in order and making sure the lender has all the information that they need to consider your loan application.

Credit Union Loans

Credit unions may not be the first place you think of when you think of small business loans, but don't overlook them. Many credit unions make loans to small businesses in their community, and during the economic downturn, some were making loans to businesses that were being turned down by other financial institutions. In addition, some credit unions offer smaller loans than some banks, and usually have very close ties to the communities in which they live and work. Some strive to lend to underserved or overlooked businesses. That makes credit unions one of the first places you may want to consider for a loan for your business.

Find out which credit unions you may be able to join at www.ASmarterChoice.org.

How to impress the lender and get the loan

A lot of borrowers are unaware of what it takes to get a business loan. They think that if they have been a regular customer of that bank, the bank should give them a loan; or if they show up with a passion about their business, the bankers will share that enthusiasm.

You will make a great impression if you know what the lender wants. We covered some of these points in the previous section on bank loans, but they are crucial so they bear repeating. Commonly, a lender is looking for the following:

- Cash Flow and Profits: Business tax returns that show two years of profitable operating history, or enough historical profits to cover your personal expenses and make a loan payment.

- Bank Accounts: Bank statements that show well-managed personal and business checking accounts—that is, no overdraft, transfers between accounts that follow sound business practices and healthy balances for business operations and household expenses.

- Credit History: Good credit history with no defaults or bankruptcies.

- Collateral: Equity in real estate, large equipment or vehicles.

- Equity: Business owner has 25% of total project costs in cash or direct investment to contribute to the project.

- Uses of funds: Funds needed to expand or evolve an already successful business.

- Industry Experience, Planning and Research: A solid business plan based on industry standards.

- Supporting Documentation: Location, job creation potential, type of business and any information that enhances the business's chances for success.

If a borrower has all of the above, they will be considered low risk and have more loan options. When one or more of the above is shaky, such as a history of overdrafts, unexplained deposits and transfers in the bank accounts, the funds are needed for business start-up or refinancing, or the business owner has little or no industry experience, then the loan application is considered to have more risk.

In the end, microlenders will go beyond what traditional banks would do in terms of risk and will be more flexible in the loan criteria. But they still have criteria. They still want to see cash flow, good management on checking accounts, some type of collateral and proof that you know your industry and how to generate revenue.

Now let's consider whether it is a good idea to use your retirement monies...

Chapter 6

Retirement Financing

Don really wanted to buy an existing franchise business. His wife Mary was less enthusiastic. Don said they needed $300,000 to get it going. The couple had explored obtaining an SBA loan but they didn't have the 25 percent down payment required. And their credit was not stellar.

The only source of money they really had was Don's 401(k) plan. He had managed to accumulate $350,000 for retirement. Mary said their financial planner warned they shouldn't take their money out for something as risky as starting a business; they would need it to help them pay expenses in their later years.

But Don felt their financial planner just wanted to hold onto their account. Of course he wouldn't suggest using the money for starting a business. He would lose out on financial planning fees.

So Don went on the internet and found all sorts of promoters claiming that one could easily tap into their 401(k) for business financing. The promoters touted that there were provisions within the Employee Retirement Income Security Act ("ERISA") and the IRS tax code allowing people to invest retirement savings in a business if they were active employees. (Those seeking passive income through absentee ownership didn't meet the requirements.)

On the internet it seemed so easy. There were five basic steps to follow:

1. <u>Set up a C corporation</u>. An S corporation, limited liability company or other structure wouldn't work. You had to set up a double tax C corporation before you created or bought your business.

2. <u>Have the C corporation set up a 401(k) plan</u>. The new plan must specifically provide for the acquisition and holding of qualified employer securities (meaning stock in the business).

3. <u>Roll your existing 401(k) plan into the new plan</u>. So your old plan gets rolled into the plan you just set up for the new C corporation.

4. <u>Have the new 401(k) invest in the new C corporation</u>. The new plan (which is specifically authorized to do so) then invests directly into the business. The plan is now a shareholder of the new C corporation.

5. <u>The 401(k) money is now in the corporation</u>. With cash in the corporate bank account you can now start doing business.

Don reported all this back to Mary. He said the unique strategy was called Rollover as Business Start-Ups or 'ROBS.' Mary was not convinced, noting that all she saw was a risky business that 'robs' their retirement monies.

Don said the promoter offered all sorts of benefits to this strategy. A key, he said, was that there was no debt service on the business like there would be with an SBA or bank loan. Their house and other assets were not exposed. While Mary acknowledged this as true, she noted that their most valuable and asset protected entity—their 401(k) plan—was now completely exposed. If the business failed their retirement monies were gone. Did Don have enough years left to ever accumulate another $300,000?

Don was confident of their future success. He noted another benefit was that all the profits went into their 401(k) plan tax free. And it would be there accumulating tax free until they needed it. Mary didn't have an answer for this and said she would talk to their CPA about it.

Several days later, Mary reported back. Their CPA was very concerned that any profits made by the C corporation were subject to taxes of between 15% and 34%.

But even worse, Mary said, were the numbers when the business was sold. Because of the double tax C corporation (the corporation being a requirement for a ROBS transaction) a great deal more in tax was paid at the time of sale.

The C corporation paid another 15% to 34% tax on the gain before money went into the 401(k) after a sale and then another hefty 10% to 39.6% personal income tax was paid when the 401(k) distributed the money out to Don. Their ROBS required a double tax scenario which robbed them of any real gains. Don thought about it all. He asked Mary what their CPA thought about ROBS plans. She said he wasn't a big fan of them. The IRS had never fully endorsed them and the Tax Court was cracking down on them. The recent case of Ellis v. Commissioner (TC Memo 2013-245) questioned the ability of taking a salary from your ROBS entity. The CPA had asked why you would set up such a convoluted structure and then not be able to take a salary from it? All in all, the CPA felt that they operated in a grey area of the IRS rules. And there were complex regulations associated with them, which if not followed, could trigger expensive penalties. Mary showed Don a few of the ongoing ROBS plan rules the CPA wrote down:

- You must operate the Plan in strict accordance with the Plan documents.

- Any full time employees of the business must be given the option to invest in subsequent employer stock offerings. (Remember the company's 401(k)—open to all employees—is the company's shareholder).

- The Plan must comply with Section 404 deduction limits if employer contributions are made.

- You must avoid any prohibited transactions. Assets of the Plan may not be used for your personal benefit. (And now salaries were targeted by the Tax Court.)

- Employer stock must be properly titled in the Plan.

- When employees participate in the plan you must obtain an ERISA bond to protect the Plan's assets.

- An annual fair market value report of ROBS Plan assets must be prepared.

- Annually, a Form 5500 must be filed to report the Plan's value and incoming contributions and rollovers.

- A Form 1099-R must be filed for outgoing transfers, rollovers or distributions.

- The Plan must be communicated to employees on an annual basis.

- The ROBS Plan document must be updated for any change in regulations.

Don just shook his head at the complexity. Mary said the CPA told her that while some promoters followed all of these rules many of the internet offerings did not, and a number of ROBS Plans were at risk as a result.

Don then asked if there were any other options for his 401(k). Mary said the CPA indicated that you could borrow up to $50,000 from a 401(k). You had to pay the money back in five years or less at an interest rate near the prime (or current standard) rate. If you ended your employment with the business that funded the plan you had to pay back the loan within 60 days or be subject to significant penalties. A Roth IRA was easier, since you could take tax free and penalty free withdrawals of all contributions that have been in the account for at least five years. But once the money was withdrawn you couldn't replace it.

Don liked the idea of borrowing at least $50,000 from his 401(k). Did the CPA see any drawbacks with that strategy?

Mary said the main drawback was that the loan had to be paid back with after tax dollars. Meaning that for each $1.00 they earned 15% was first taken out in Federal taxes. (State taxes could increase that amount.) So the 401(k) loan was paid back with 85 cent dollars. Then, when you pulled money out of your 401(k) you had to pay a 15% tax (or whatever your rate was at the time) again. With the two taxes involved, the loan eventually cost 60 cents for each dollar used. Because you were voluntarily paying the twin taxes, the CPA called it 'personal predatory lending.'

But if that's what it took, Don thought, so be it. He would find a smaller business to start and borrow $50,000 from his 401(k).

The ROBS Plan, for many, is too complicated and risky. For others, it is the only way forward. Their money is in their 401(k) and those are the only funds available. The key is to be very clear about it all. Your monies are asset protected in a 401(k). Creditors cannot reach them. When you pull the money out you lose that protection. There are ongoing requirements to meet. The IRS has not fully sanctioned the ROBS Plan and the Tax Court is limiting their effectiveness. Spouses will have some pertinent, and perhaps piercing, comments about their use.

Let's look at another, even riskier, retirement money strategy for financing a real estate investment...

The Checkbook IRA

When you have money in your IRA (Individual Retirement Account) you can make a wider range of investments than you can with a 401(k). You can invest, for example, in real estate, mortgages, tax liens, joint ventures, stocks you select and certain precious metals. The IRS doesn't allow IRA investments into artwork, rugs, antiques, gems, stamps and the like.

When you want to have more control in directing these investments you can set up a self-directed IRA account whereby a custodian or trustee helps you manage the account and file all the required IRS reports.

The trustee will also help you steer clear of the many prohibited transactions set forth by the IRS. These are self-dealing or conflict of interest transactions which benefit the IRA holder or other disqualified persons (think family members) and not the IRA account.

If you are caught in a prohibited transaction, your IRA account is treated as being distributed. This means penalties and interest are owed, which can whittle your IRA account down to zero. Not good retirement planning.

Prohibited transactions include:
- Borrowing money from the IRA
- Selling property to the IRA
- Compensation for managing it
- Using the IRA as security for a personal loan
- Personally guaranteeing an IRA loan

- Personal use of IRA owned property
- Providing services to an IRA investment, including real estate services

The last prohibited transaction has led to a great deal of confusion. If your IRA invests in a single family home you rent out to tenants, can you go in and fix a toilet? More broadly, with an IRA can you be involved in 'Active Landlording?' The rules consider that a prohibited transaction—you are providing services directly to your IRA plan.

To stay within the rules you must have your self-directed IRA trustee hire a plumber to fix the toilet. So not only do you have to pay the plumber but you have to pay the trustee to pay for the plumber.

Into this vortex the promoters of Checkbook IRAs (also called Checkbook LLCs) have arisen.

Their pitch is simple. Instead of paying the trustee for every transaction, you set up an LLC owned by the IRA. Then you are manager of the LLC and get to write checks for it. (Hence, Checkbook IRA.) In doing so, you can save on all the trustee fees.

It sounds great. But there is one big problem.

If you can't write checks for your self-directed IRA plan (which you absolutely cannot!) then how can you write checks for the LLC owned by the IRA? Aren't you personally managing your IRA monies? Aren't you personally providing services to your IRA by managing its money?

Of course you are.

And then what if you need to put money into the LLC account? Once you've funded the LLC it becomes a disqualified entity. Any additional outside monies you put into it are a prohibited transaction. Oops. All the penalties and interest now owed have wiped out your IRA account.

Equity Trust Company is one of the nation's largest self-directed IRA trustees. They know the law and won't accept Checkbook IRA arrangements. Jeff Desich is the CEO of Equity Trust. Jeff states, "I strongly believe there is a tremendous risk with using the Checkbook IRA scheme."

If that admonition is not enough, consider the issues on the administration of the account. With the Checkbook IRA you are now the custodian, you are now responsible for maintaining all the paperwork associated with the file, and responsible for any mistakes that are made. If you get audited will your paperwork stand up?

The safer course is to stay away from Checkbook IRAs.

As well, as our 401(k) example illustrated, if you have to use IRA monies you may be just better off pulling the money out, paying the tax and 10% penalty and moving on. Once the money is outside the IRA you can take advantage of the real estate tax write offs (i.e. depreciation) that make such investments truly beneficial to the bottom line.

So overall, we are not big fans of using retirement monies to fund a business.

By starting your own business, you are taking a lot of risk. The odds are already stacked against you. Your retirement plans are generally protected against creditors. That means, even in the worse-case scenario where you file for bankruptcy, you will likely be able to keep the money you stashed away in your 401(k), IRA, or pension plan. By cashing it out or borrowing against it, you are taking safe money and turning it into very risky money. Also, if you don't make your payments as agreed, the loan is then considered a withdrawal and you will likely pay taxes and penalties. Let's consider another option.

Life Insurance Loans

If you have a life insurance policy with cash value (whole or universal life), borrowing against it should be easy. There is no credit check, the loan generally doesn't have to be repaid (with caveats below), and the interest rate is usually low.

But there are a couple of possible pitfalls. One is that borrowing against the policy will reduce the benefit to your heirs if you die before the loan is paid back. Make sure you still have enough life insurance. If needed, supplement with a term policy.

The other drawback is that interest will be charged, and if you don't pay it back, there could be serious consequences. You can instruct the insurer to pay the interest from dividends or from the remaining cash value of your policy, but you may not realize how high the balance has risen. If there is not enough cash value or dividends to cover the loan, your policy could lapse.

Even worse, you may find your owe taxes on the amount you borrowed—plus unpaid interest! Why? Because the insurer is giving you a loan with your insurance policy as collateral. (You aren't really withdrawing the cash value of your policy; you are borrowing against it.) If you die and the proceeds cover the loan plus interest, your beneficiaries will receive anything that remains. But if the amount you owe (including interest) exceeds your cash value, or if you let the policy lapse or cancel it with a loan outstanding while you are still alive, you run into something called Cancellation of Indebtedness Income.

When you borrow money and don't pay it back, the IRS considers that cancelled debt taxable income, and the total amount of "income" can include interest that accumulated but was not repaid. So if you cancel the policy or let it lapse before you repay the loan, the IRS will expect you to include that amount in your income when you prepare your return. Forgiveness of debt is income.

To be safe, you'll want to watch your policy closely. Make sure you are working with a knowledgeable agent who understands these risks, and consider paying the interest if failing to do so will put you at risk of owing taxes to the IRS.

Life insurance loans don't show up on credit reports, however. In that sense, this can be an excellent way to borrow without affecting your credit scores.

Now let's explore some specialized strategies…

Chapter 7

Special Financing

EB-5 visa

Marriott International wanted to open a new $88 million hotel in downtown Seattle in 2008. It was not a good time to look for money for any sort of real estate development, much less a hospitality project. With financing dried up and the travel industry in free-fall, new hotels were definitely out of favor during the downturn.

But the desire to become a U.S. citizen remained strong. So Marriott used a funding mechanism which allows wealthy immigrants to obtain a green card and residency in exchange for investing in the United States: the EB-5 program.

The EB-5 program grants visas to foreigners who invest at least $500,000 in an American business that creates at least 10 new jobs.

Hotels are an excellent fit for this type of funding since they need people—housekeepers, desk clerks and the like—to operate the business. Marriott also used the EB-5 visa program to build a 377 room hotel near the Staples Center, the home arena for four professional sports franchises in downtown Los Angeles. The project's goal, in keeping with the employment requirement, was to create 3360 direct and indirect jobs. It is on track to create employment for 4,240 people. Is it worth allowing 1336 wealthy foreign individuals to become U.S. citizens in exchange for generating thousands of jobs?

Many think so. And many countries now have similar programs, including Canada, New Zealand, Australia and Britain. The lion's share of EB-5 visas are granted to Chinese individuals who are seeking political freedom and economic opportunity. Citizens from India, Taiwan, South Korea and Canada are also using the program to gain entry into the United States.

With Marriott leading the way, a number of hotel chains, such as Hilton, Hyatt and Starwood are using EB-5 financing. Hotel developers can offer returns of 4% or less, far lower than traditional financing. Of course, the foreigners are buying a visa and are less concerned with a rate of return on their investment. Indeed, their key return is admittance into the country.

To qualify, individuals must invest $1,000,000 (or $500,000 for a rural or high unemployment area) while creating or preserving at least 10 jobs. The investor and their immediate family do not count towards the worker requirement, even if they work in the business. The process starts with an EB-5 petition, which features an economist's report showing how the project will create employment, as well as information demonstrating that the monies to be invested are clean, noncriminal funds. (Drug lords and warlords are not allowed.) The petition can take two to six months to get approved. The investor then applies for an immigrant visa (or green card) which can take another four to six months. With a green card the investor can become a conditional permanent resident of the United States. Their spouse and children under age 21 can also obtain green cards.

The green cards are valid for two years. Before the two years are up the investor files a 'Petition to Remove Conditions' showing that the investment has been made and the jobs have been created. Upon approval, the investor then obtains a permanent green card. If desired, the investor can apply for U.S. citizenship.

There are service providers and law firms available to guide foreign investors through this process.

Keep in mind there is some risk for the investor. If their investment doesn't pan out and the jobs aren't created, their permanent green card will not be forthcoming. Investors need good counsel and good projects.

Could your business opportunity be one of the good projects? Why not? You don't have to be a large hotel chain to take advantage of this funding mechanism.

Suppose you are starting a restaurant or a retail store or a high tech start-up. You need $500,000 to get started and your business plan calls for the hiring of ten American employees. You have wealthy cousins in Holland (or Dubai, or wherever). They want their newly married child with their newly born grandchild to grow up in the United States and attend an American university. With a year of advance planning, an EB-5 visa petition is filed and the money invested in your new business. Your cousins obtain their green cards and can live wherever they want in the U.S.A. (Meaning that they don't have to live in the same city as the business they invested in is located.)

What if, like most of us, you don't have wealthy cousins overseas? You may then want to consider contacting a Regional Center, chartered by the U.S. Citizenship and Immigration Service. These Regional Centers—some of which are private enterprises, others which are regional government agencies— assist in accepting EB-5 capital for economic development in the United States. These centers may (or may not, depending on their charter) be able to assist you in getting your business funded.

As we've discussed, the process can take up to a year to complete. Beware of promoters claiming it can be done more quickly. Also know that the foreign investor will be investing not only money but their family's future on your business success. If you don't want that kind of pressure to perform you may want to consider another funding avenue.

SBIR Grants: Prove it

Have you heard of SBIR grants? Not many have, but they can be an excellent way to prove up your idea or technology.

The Small Business Innovation Research (or SBIR) program is a federal government initiative administered by the Small Business Administration. The idea is to encourage small U.S. businesses to pursue research and development (R&D) projects that have the potential for commercialization. Each year, federal agencies with extramural R&D budgets exceeding $100 million are required to allocate 2.5% of their budget to SBIR grants. As of this writing, eleven federal agencies are involved:

- National Aeronautics and Space Administration (NASA)
- National Science Foundation
- Department of Agriculture
- Department of Commerce – National Institute of Standards and Technology
- Department of Commerce – National Oceanic and Atmospheric Administration
- Department of Defense
- Department of Education
- Department of Energy
- Department of Health and Human Services

- Department of Homeland Security
- Department of Transportation
- Environmental Protection Agency

SBIR's mission is to advance technological innovation, or as program founder Roland Tibbets stated: "To provide funding for some of the best early-stage innovation ideas—ideas that, however promising, are still too high risk for private investors, including venture capital firms."

SBIR's stated goals are to:

- Stimulate technological innovation
- Meet Federal research and development needs
- Foster and encourage participation in innovation and entrepreneurship by socially and economically disadvantaged persons
- Increase private-sector commercialization of innovations derived from Federal research and development funding.

Only U.S. small businesses may participate in the SBIR grant program. You must have no more than 500 employees and your company must be:

- Organized for profit, with a place of business located in the United States;
- At least 51% owned and controlled by one or more individuals who are citizens of, or permanent resident aliens in, the United States; or
- At least 51% owned and controlled by another for-profit business concern that is at least 51% owned and controlled by one or more individuals who are citizens of, or permanent resident aliens in, the United States.

If your company qualifies then you may participate in SBIR's three phase program.

Phase I

The purpose of Phase I is to both 1) prove the commercial potential and technical merit of an idea and/or technology and 2) demonstrate the company's ability to perform and reach goals. Phase I awards are generally up to $150,000 for about six months' worth of support.

Phase II

Phase II's objective is to then continue and expand the R&D efforts and to further evaluate commercialization potential. Grants in Phase II are up to $1 million for as many as 2 years of support. Phase II grants are only awarded to Phase I winners (although Phase I winners may jump straight to Phrase III).

Phase III

Phase III is when the idea leaves the laboratory and enters the marketplace. At this point there are no further SBIR grants (although some non-SBIR federal funding may be available). Generally, however, the business has proved the concept and is ready to seek private funding.

As of this writing the SBIR program has provided over $2 billion a year in grants and contracts to small U.S. businesses. Of the 11 federal agencies involved half of the money, or $1 billion, is awarded by the Department of Defense ("DOD"). SBIR grants were used by the DOD to develop their unmanned aerial vehicle devices, now commonly known as drones. This technology has provided employment opportunities for many, not the least of which are all the constitutional lawyers, paralegals and scholars who must sort out the attendant privacy and ethical issues over the next several decades regarding drones flying over your back yard.

The SBIR program as a whole has had some notable success stories. Companies including Qualcomm, Symantec, iRobot and DaVinci were started with R&D funding from SBIR programs.

By now you are asking: What is the catch? Well, the private companies own all the intellectual property and all commercialization rights created under the program. That is, of course, good for you. The only catch with a SBIR grant is that the program is highly selective and competitive. This is to be expected from a government program that gives out free money to help visionaries become multi-millionaires.

As mentioned, the U.S. Small Business Administration coordinates the SBIR program. They can be reached at:

U.S. Small Business Administration
Office of Technology
409 Third Street, SW
Washington, DC 20416
(202) 205-6450
www.sbir.gov

In terms of other special and creative financing opportunities, Tom Wheelwright, the Rich Dad Advisor, CPA and author of *Tax-Free Wealth* also shares his insights:

There are many creative ways to finance your existing business. While many people often look to banks, family, friends and their own personal savings, there are a number of other sources for cash flow to improve your business. Here are a few of our favorites.

At the top of the list is creating new sales. Look for ways you can increase your sales through marketing partners, affiliates, and the internet. Or look at ways to increase your sales closing ratio from your current sales force. Years ago I took some terrific sales training and ever since then, if I ever need some more money, I add my own sales skills to those of my sales force and go out and sell services myself. This isn't the best use of my time for the long term, but it can provide a needed cash infusion in the short term.

The fastest and easiest way to increase your cash flow is to reduce your taxes. Most business owners will pay anywhere from a third to a half or more of their net income in employment and income taxes. A good tax strategy can typically reduce this figure by 10-40%. Your tax strategy should include a look at what entity holds your business and how that entity is taxed, what additional deductions you can get that you aren't currently taking, and even ways to produce nontaxable income. A good tax advisor can help you develop a long-term tax strategy in three months or less and much of the tax savings will come in the first month.

Another source of financing is to get your customers to pay more quickly. You can do this with incentives or penalties. I personally prefer the incentives, as they not only accelerate your cash flow but they also improve your customer relations. An example of this strategy is to give your customers a discount if they pay within 10 days of receiving your invoice. You may have heard of a 2/10 net 30 invoice strategy. This means you give them a 2% discount if they pay within 10 days, otherwise they have to pay you the full amount owed within 30 days to stay current with their account.

If you do provide penalties for late payment, be sure to be consistent and ALWAYS assess the penalty. The worst thing you can do is tell them that you are going to charge interest of 1.5% per month and then not charge it. Or, say that they will be a 5% penalty for late payment and then let them off the hook. Maintaining and enforcing your strategy consistently will be critical. Otherwise, your customers will quickly learn that it's okay to pay late and you may begin seeing customers who paid on time begin paying late as a way to manage their own cash flow.

This brings me to the next strategy for increasing your cash flow and that is to delay payment to your vendors. I would not make this a long-term strategy as it will strain your relationship with your vendors. However, most vendors will understand if you need some extra time during a down cycle in your business and will give you the time to pay without penalty.

Thanks Tom. Now let's look at a traditional and ever popular method of financing...

Chapter 8

Seller Financing

Chad wanted to start an automobile repair business. He knew the industry and had worked his way up from mechanic to supervisor. But there were no opportunities for further growth. The owner wouldn't make him a partner, and Chad realized he was too much like the owner. He wanted to own and control his own business.

Chad looked into starting a new auto repair business from scratch. He would have to lease a new space, buy tools and equipment and then heavily advertise to get new customers.

Chad's wife Ruth did not like this idea. There was too much risk. What if the customers didn't come? What if they didn't like his new location? Ruth had over a hundred 'what ifs' for why a start-up may not work. Chad wasn't overly pleased by all her questions, but deep down he knew they were the right things to ask.

But then Ruth came up with a 'what if' that sounded very good to Chad.

What if he bought an existing business?

That made a great deal of sense to both Chad and Ruth. They would buy existing customers, a well-known 'brand' with an established location and actual revenue.

With that, Chad and Ruth began searching the internet for auto repair businesses for sale. They found one in the next town over that Chad had heard about over the years.

Alpine Auto had a good reputation in the area and a loyal following. The proprietor had suddenly passed and his surviving spouse, Nora, was at a loss on how to run the business.

Chad and Ruth met with Nora and her attorney and it seemed like a good fit. Until one hiccup almost killed the deal.

Chad and Ruth's credit was not stellar. They had bought a house at the top of the market and had been forced to walk away from it. While their credit was recovering they could not obtain a loan for the full purchase price of $400,000 for the business. They had a fund of $100,000 from various accounts and a pledge of help from Chad's father, but that was it.

Chad, Ruth and Nora were all very sorry the deal wasn't coming together. It was the perfect opportunity for Chad and Ruth, and it got Nora out of a business she had no idea how to run. But then the attorney made a two word suggestion that appealed to all three of them:

SELLER FINANCING

The attorney explained that seller financing happened all the time in real estate. You buy a property and pay the former owner back pursuant to a promissory note. In real estate it is called 'carrying the paper' and the seller gets paid back over time. It also works with business assets.

The attorney explained that Nora could accept a 20% down payment of $80,000 and a promissory note of $320,000 at a 6% interest rate. Chad and Ruth would pay Nora (instead of their own bank) $4,678 a month for seven years. Once the note was paid, the extra cash flow was theirs to keep. In this scenario, Chad and Ruth could get into the business, and still have $20,000 for working capital (their $100,000 fund less the

$80,000 down payment to Nora). Nora's promissory note would be secured by a UCC-1 financing statement giving Nora first rights to all the equipment and business assets if there was a default on the note.

Nora was the bank in this sale. Like a bank, if Chad and Ruth didn't make the monthly payments she would get the collateral back—Alpine Auto. Of course she didn't want it back. She didn't know how to run it and she wanted to slow down after her husband's passing. She also wanted the cash flow of $4,678 a month for the next seven years. So Nora had an incentive to make sure the deal worked. To that end, she agreed to help with the transition for the next six months. She agreed to introduce Chad and Ruth to Alpine's best customers and service providers. While not specifically agreed to but arising solely out of the situation, Nora spoke very highly of Chad and Ruth as the successors of her late husband's devotion to customer service. And the customers and vendors who liked Nora and her late husband knew exactly what was happening. They wanted Nora to retire in comfort and agreed to keep coming (for now) to Alpine Auto. Chad and Ruth would have to prove themselves as dependable and honest in future years. But for now, to help Nora, the customers would continue to use Alpine Auto.

The deal was struck. Chad and Ruth bought Alpine Auto with seller financing. Nora, the seller, was the financier as well. Chad and Ruth made the payments like clockwork every month. All parties benefitted.

Have you thought about buying an existing business? There are a lot of advantages to it: A track record, existing customers and actual revenue.

Operating businesses are sold every day. And like Chad and Ruth's case illustrates, many of these business sales feature a way for you to get into them: Seller financing.

A seller of a business takes a down payment (usually of 20% or more) and extends a loan to you, the buyer of the business, for the remainder of the purchase price. You then make installment payments (usually on a monthly basis) over a fixed term at a fixed interest rate until the loan is repaid. The seller is in effect your bank. And like a bank, they can take the business back if you don't make the payments.

Also like a bank, the seller is going to be very concerned about your creditworthiness, as well as your integrity and ability to pay. The last thing a seller wants to do is come back and run a company they wanted to be free from, a company you may have wrecked while you owned it. So expect the seller to be very cautious, which is entirely appropriate. That said, with lending restrictions imposed on banks after the 2008 collapse, seller financing has become a key factor in business sale transactions.

As a buyer of the business beware of notes calling for balloon payments, where a large amount of money is due at the end of a certain period. Monthly payments for two or three years followed by a very large payment may not give you enough time to advance the business. You may not have enough of a track record to refinance the loan.

For example, you buy a business for $1,000,000 with a $250,000 down payment. Your monthly payments on the $750,000 note at 8% interest amortized (stretched out) are $6,273.50. You can handle that for two years. But the balloon payment at the start of the third year means you owe the seller a lump sum payment of $696,768.66. Sure, you can use more financing to pay off the first note. But will you be able to get such a loan? Be realistic.

You can certainly ask the seller to accept contingency payments. This entails setting goals for the business. You pay the seller a certain amount at closing and perhaps payments pursuant to a note. But you also pay the seller monies if the business hits certain profit goals. When the seller has a stake in the profits they are more likely to be helpful towards the new management.

In some cases, the seller may also take stock in the buyer's new company. If the seller believes in you and your team and sees a profitable future ahead, a portion of the purchase price may be accepted in stock. While you are giving up a percentage of ownership, at the start you have just printed out a share certificate, a piece of paper. It can feel better than a full on monthly payment obligation.

A seller may also take convertible securities as payment. In this way, the seller offers the buyer a note or loan that, at the end of the loan's life, may be converted by the seller into company stock. The benefit to the seller is that he or she has the opportunity of owning stock—with hopefully a future upside potential—in the company, while still having an income source for the initial years during the loan life. The benefit to the buyer is it allows them to acquire the business and keep the seller incentivized and interested in its success.

All these options relate to the basic interrelation of price and terms. Don't get stuck on the price when you get what you need by better terms. Sellers get better sales prices when they offer terms. A recent study found that partially-financed sales result in sales prices that were 15% higher than a cash sale. As a business buyer, know this correlation. So if a seller insists on $1 million dollars, offer terms that allow you to get into the business on favorable terms. The seller eventually gets their price but they get paid over a period of years without sacrificing all your capital upfront. If the seller is fixed on price, use the terms of payment to your advantage. Conversely, if the seller is stuck on more favorable terms, offer a lower price to swing the deal. The correlation between price and terms clearly exists. Use it to your advantage.

Another advantage of this approach: As a buyer, you know that seller financing means that the seller is not afraid for the future of the business. The seller who will only nervously accept an all cash offer may know of some industry disruption headed down the tracks. Why buy an injection molding company when inexpensive 3-D printers are ready to hit the market? The seller may have a crystal ball they are not sharing with you. They want all cash because they can see what's coming and they want a clean getaway. As a buyer, use this argument to your advantage. Also use the fact that the seller gains a tax advantage by accepting an installment sale. This method stretches out any capital gains. Talk to your CPA about the advantages of installment sales, and use the benefits in your discussions with the seller.

The most common form of security for a seller financing transaction is a personal guarantee by the buyer and the buyer's spouse. If the buyer doesn't make the payments their personal assets, including their personal residence, are at risk. Sellers expect a personal guarantee. They want your skin in the game. If your spouse is unwilling to sign such a document you may have trouble reaching a closing.

Another form of security, as was mentioned in Chad and Ruth's case, is the UCC-1 financing statement. This is a form filed with your county recorder's office or secretary of state's office providing notice of a security interest in specific assets.

The seller retains a priority (or first dibs) to assets such as equipment, intellectual property, accounts receivable and the like. UCC-1s are also discussed in Chapter Four of Garrett Sutton's book *Start Your Own Corporation*. A seller will (or should) insist on the security of a UCC-1 in any seller financing transaction.

Specific collateral may also exist in the form of first or second deeds of trust against any real estate involved in the sale. As well, a personal guarantee may be secured by a second deed of trust against the buyer's home or other real estate holdings.

A seller may also secure their loan with a 'stock pledge.' The buyer forms a corporation to run the business and grants the seller the right to vote the stock in certain circumstances. If the note is not honored the seller can step in to vote that payments are made or, in extreme cases, take even more drastic measures to get paid. Restrictions on how the business is run can be included in any sale agreement as well. The maintenance of key operating ratios and limits on the new owners' paycheck are common restrictions. All of this is standard for business acquisitions where the seller 'carries the paper.'

Seller financing may not be palatable to every seller but it does offer one clear advantage: A faster close. With the seller acting as the bank a decision is quickly made. On the other hand, traditional banks may take a long time to reject loan applications for business acquisitions and even longer to process the small percentage they will accept.

As a buyer asking for seller financing you can also mention that banks frequently provide the buyer with negative feedback about the business to be acquired. Many bankers have killed many deals in this fashion. You can hear them say: "You're going to buy what?" Magnanimously make the seller aware of this risk.

As you might imagine, having a business attorney with experience in company sales is very important. There are many pitfalls to overcome and a good attorney can help you around them. For more information on these and related issues please see Garrett's book, *Buying & Selling a Business*.

Now let's consider another commonly used strategy...

CHAPTER 9

Equipment Leasing

When starting a business you have to ask: Do I need to buy every-thing to get started? The reason we ask this question is that the less you have to buy outright, the less money you may need at the start (or in the middle). That is where equipment leasing comes into play. If we can lease the equipment we need at an affordable monthly cost we can get started more quickly and easily. Equipment leasing is another form of business financing.

As such, the question of whether to buy or lease equipment is a common one for business startups. There is no one-size-fits-all answer. Every business must take into account its unique needs, opportunities, and challenges, but there are a few considerations to take into account that will help make the decision-making a little easier.

Leasing equipment can help a business grow more rapidly, enabling it to operate with better equipment at lower monthly costs. That equipment can be earning the company money before the company has the money to buy it outright.

Types of Equipment Leases

Most equipment leases can be broken down into two basic types: short-term and long-term. Know that there are a variety of other lease arrangements available.

Short-term leases, also known as operating leases, usually have cancelable terms without major penalties. Such leases are often desirable for businesses with short-term equipment needs. The lessor (the one leasing out the equipment) bears the obsolescence risk of a short-term lease, which is usually small due to the short timeframe of the lease. Companies needing equipment for only short periods of time or needing high-tech equipment that always needs to be upgraded may benefit from short-term leases.

Long-term leases, also known as capital leases, financial leases, or full payout leases, are not easy to cancel. Such leases offer a way to finance assets and are usually net leases. A net lease holds that the lessee, the party leasing the equipment, is responsible for the maintenance, insurance, and applicable taxes on the equipment. Companies needing equipment for use for long periods of time may benefit from long-term leases. This is especially true in the case of expensive equipment that may be harder to pay for outright. A good example of a net lease is for a copier. Most every business needs the marvel that can copy, scan, fax and collate. To buy one outright is a stretch. To lease one over many months is eminently doable.

When entering into an equipment lease be sure to read the contract. Better yet, have your attorney review it as well. Be on the lookout for the following terms:

1. How long the lease will last
2. How much the lessor will be paid
3. Terms of payment
4. Residual values and purchase options
5. Market value of equipment
6. Tax responsibility
7. Provision for updating or canceling
8. Options for renewing
9. Penalties for canceling early in cases where there isn't good cause

10. Security deposits, warranties, and other miscellaneous items

Please be very aware of the $1.00 buyout option. When you lease the equipment for, say, five years, you may have the option to buy it for $1.00 after 60 months. But if you keep paying the monthly lease most companies won't remind you that with just a dollar buyout you could be out of the lease. Pay attention to the time frames of the lease.

Lease rates can vary among companies, even for the same piece of equipment. These variations can be substantial, so be sure to check around. Some terms are within the lessee's control, some aren't. Factors include:

1. The policies of the particular lease company
2. Lessee credit history
3. Nature of equipment
4. Length of lease of term
5. The primary beneficiary of tax credits

Advantages of Leasing Over Buying

Convenience

Acquiring equipment can be a hassle. More precisely, it can be a series of hassles—negotiating price, arranging proper insurance, providing proper registration, negotiating resale or arranging for disposal, canceling insurance, transferring registration. Setting up a lease agreement can be a fast and inexpensive alternative when there isn't time to go through the loan application process or when equipment is only going to be needed for a limited time.

Reduced Initial Expense

Equipment leases seldom include a down payment, nor do they tie up available lines of credit, making them attractive to businesses with tight cash flow. Necessary equipment can be acquired with minimal upfront cash outlay through the judicious use of leases.

Flexibility

The flexibility of lease terms compared to loans include no down payment (keeping operating capital and borrowing capacity open), options to spread payments over longer periods of time, and consideration of the financing as an operating expense (not a liability, and thus keeping it off the balance sheet).

Budgeting

Spreading equipment costs out over many months through a lease, especially a lease that allows for upgrading that equipment, simplifies a company's budget. Because lease payments frequently do not require a down payment, many companies choose to lease higher quality equipment than they could afford to buy. In this way, leasing reduces the incidence of unexpected expenditures.

Upgrades

Leasing is a particularly handy way of dealing with obsolescence in high-tech equipment. A business can lease a high-end computer system, for example, and not worry if it needs to be upgraded in three years. The burden of obsolescence is on the lessor. The business can simply lease new and better equipment when the lease is up—with no worries about what to do with the old and no regret over the low resale value.

Maintenance

In a lease, the lessor remains the owner of the equipment and has a vested interest in keeping that equipment in good condition.

Many, though not all, equipment lease agreements include maintenance. Even if maintenance increases the monthly payments associated with the lease, it can save the lessee money. The lessee may get a discount on replacement parts and labor costs—all of which would not readily be available to a lessee otherwise. And beyond the cost savings, the peace of mind that comes with not having to worry about or deal with maintenance of equipment can be crucial for a hectic and harried startup.

Tax deductions

Lease payments are a business expense and can be deducted as such on the company's tax return. This needs to be taken into consideration when calculating the net cost of the lease.

Disadvantages of Leasing Over Buying

Lack of Ownership

For equipment with a long useful life and a low likelihood of obsolescence, ownership has significant advantages, equity and full control of the asset being the top two. With an equipment lease, the lessee does not own the equipment, and cannot benefit from a resale value from that equipment. Similarly, only the equipment owner (the lessor) can claim the deduction of the asset at tax time.

Long-Term Costs

When calculated over a period of years, leasing is often more expensive than buying outright. When comparing costs, it is important to take into consideration deposits, interest, and monthly payments. Low monthly payments can be very attractive for a startup, but they add up quickly.

Rigidity

When you sign a lease you are locked into payments for the whole lease period, even if you no longer need or use the equipment. There is nothing more frustrating than writing a lease payment for a clunky computer system gathering dust in the closet. If your lease terms allow for cancellation you may have some flexibility. But those cancellation options, like most options, will come with fees.

Complexity

A lease agreement is a contract, and a contract is a legal document. An outright purchase can be much more straightforward and less complex. A purchase can certainly be easier to manage than a lease, assuming it is a cash purchase and not done with a loan or on credit.

Lease Checklist

The following are some questions to take into consideration when making the decision to lease or buy equipment:
- What do you need to run your business?
- How long will you be needing the equipment?
- Do you want to handle training yourself or have the equipment supplier do it for you?
- Where will you be getting supplies (do you want supplies to be part of your lease)?
- What will the total monthly payments be?
- What will the total balance be by the end of the lease term?
- Who will be your contact at the leasing company?
- How long has the leasing company been around?

- Who will be financing your lease (is it a separate company)?
- What, if any, insurance is included as part of your lease?
- What taxes are included as part of your lease?
- Are repairs covered in the lease?
- Can you upgrade the equipment?
- Can you trade in the equipment?

Equipment leasing is a beneficial arrangement for many business owners. Because it is so popular there are many unscrupulous operators in the marketplace out to defraud you. We have included some cautionary comments in Chapter 19 on Scams.

But otherwise, besides knowing what to look out for (and to avoid), equipment leasing will be an excellent tool in your business financing tool kit. Many entrepreneurs before you have used it to their advantage.

Now let's factor in another unique strategy...

Chapter 10

Factoring and Merchant Cash Advances

Roger and Carol faced financial ruin. They were doing so well, and yet...

The two ran a company that provided unique locking bolts to advanced manufacturing firms. All their high tech customers loved their product. But they couldn't get paid from their big company clients in a timely manner to keep the doors open.

They were owed $200,000 for bolts they had produced and shipped. But they owed $30,000 immediately to their suppliers, employees and landlord. Their accounts receivable (the money others owed them) was not coming in fast enough to cover their accounts payable (the money they owed others).

They called their CPA for advice. For the first time ever they learned about factoring. A factor, explained the CPA, was a person or company who bought accounts receivable at a discount. This allowed Roger and Carol to get money in the door to pay their various expenses, and thus keep the doors open.

The CPA used one of their larger accounts receivable as an example. A Fortune 500 company, a large organization with billions of dollars in assets, owed Roger and Carol $50,000. While there was little question they would get paid—it was a billion dollar company—the wait was killing them. The CPA said a factor would buy the receivable for 70% to 85% of the amount owed. At 75% of the $50,000 receivable, the factor would pay Roger and Carol $37,500 right away. The factor would then collect the full $50,000 when the large company finally paid several months later. That would do the trick. The discounted receivable would provide the $30,000 they needed immediately to keep going.

How Factoring Works

There are three parties to a factoring transaction. The first is the one with the account receivable, or the seller. The second is the debtor, the customer of the seller. The third is the factor, the one who buys the receivable at a discount and receives the full amount of the invoice at a later date.

The sale of the receivable transfers ownership of it from the seller to the factor. In most cases, though not all, the factor notifies the debtor of the transfer, invoices the debtor and is paid directly by the debtor.

In non-recourse factoring, the factor takes the risk that the debtor doesn't pay the bill. For this type of factoring, the factors prefer to participate in factoring transactions involving large, well-established companies. A Fortune 500 company is much less of a risk than a newly established business down the street with no credit history. As such, the factor doesn't care so much about your credit history. They care about the debtor's credit history—the business they (hopefully) are going to collect from.

Not all invoices can be factored. If a small company without a solid track record is behind on payments to you, for example, you'll need to hire a collection firm, not a factoring firm. And to factor accounts receivable, the work or service must have been completed, or the product already sold. You can't factor prospective sales. (However, a merchant cash advance may be an option in some situations. More on that in a moment.)

Invoice discounting is another form of factoring though it works slightly differently. Here, the invoice serves as collateral for a short-term loan and payment will be collected from the business that provided the goods or services. Again, it can be fast, but it can also be more expensive—much more expensive—than a short-term loan.

Choosing the right factoring firm is important. Some specialize in certain types of businesses; medical, telecom, transportation or construction companies, for example. Others specialize in working with small businesses. You'll want to check out the company's history and background, and of course make sure they are a good fit for your business.

Personal guarantees on factored transactions vary. Of course, for the business owner the ideal situation will be to factor an invoice with no personal guaranty required, and that is usually the case. But sometimes the contract will require the owner to sign a personal guaranty to protect the firm against fraud or misrepresentation, or it may require a full personal guaranty if the invoice that was factored cannot be collected.

Advantages of Factoring

Factoring can provide life-saving liquidity to business owners. For one thing, it can provide cash very quickly for those in a cash crunch. Funding can take place in as little as 24 hours for a business that has established a relationship with a factor. Otherwise it may take a week or so to get started. That's light years faster than trying to get a loan or raise money on a crowdfunding platform, for example.

And because the factor is most concerned about the credit-worthiness of the debtor (the company that owes money on an invoice), it is not out of reach for a startup with no established track record.

Factoring receivables can also be an asset protection strategy. Once the assets are factored, they are no longer assets of the company, which can reduce your company's exposure, provided of course, that the proceeds have been spent or distributed.

A factor can alleviate you and your business of the headaches of tracking and trying to collect all of the company's receivables.

Disadvantages of Factoring

You have to be very cautious. For example, Walmart is well known for not paying its vendors for several months. It is said that Walmart makes as much money on its 'float' as it does selling products. That is, by holding onto monies owed to others for as long as possible they can earn interest on that floating money reserve. How much interest could you earn by holding onto many billions of dollars for a few extra months? It should be noted that what Walmart does here is not illegal or improper. If you want that massive order from Walmart those are the terms, take it or leave it.

The problem arises when you try and factor the Walmart receivable. A factor will certainly take it on. They're Walmart. The factor will surely be paid. But you may find there is no room for your company to make a profit. First off, Walmart's huge order will likely leave you with a razor thin margin. They will grind you on the price knowing you want their mammoth order. But if you're not careful, that margin may not be enough to cover the factor's discounts. A number of companies have lost a large amount of money and/or gone out of business when they slashed their profits to get the business from large companies like Walmart and then didn't have enough room to factor the receivable. So talk to your factor about terms before you accept that gigantic order (both in terms of volume and challenge).

The cost of factoring is often not apparent since it is not expressed as an interest rate.

Factors do take on their own risks in these transactions. They can become involved in contractual disputes where the debtor refuses to pay the seller (and thus the factor). There are tax and legal risks associated with complying with all the laws and regulations in various countries. As well, some sellers are engaged in active fraud towards the factor. Fake invoicing, un-assigned credit notes and misdirected payments are just some of the pitfalls facing a factor. They often earn their fees.

Despite the risks, factoring has been around for a very long time. Of the 282 rules etched into the human sized stone that is Hammurabi's Code, that incredible rock of law from 1772 BC, rules on factoring are included. From ancient Babylon to today, factoring is an established means of providing needed and timely liquidity to growing businesses.

Merchant Cash Advances

Merchant cash advances (a form of revenue-based financing) are similar to factoring in some respects, but they are a different product. Unlike factoring, where a company essentially sells invoices for products or services already delivered, merchant cash advances allow a company to get cash based on anticipated sales in the future. For example, a restaurant that needs to purchase some special equipment might get a cash advance against future credit card sales.

These have become very popular over the past few years as traditional lenders cut back on business loans. For one thing they are fast: funding can come through in a matter of days. Plus, credit isn't usually a factor. Instead, the company providing this service is looking primarily at sales, and the likelihood that those sales will continue.

As with factoring, there are risks to the companies that provide merchant cash advances. If the company they front money to goes under, or if sales tank, they don't get paid. For that reason, expect some due diligence when you apply for an advance. Do your due diligence as well, to make sure you are dealing with a reputable company that understands your business—and one that isn't charging you an arm and a leg. After all, this is your future cash flow you're talking about and if you're not careful, a merchant cash advance can be like a payday loan that traps you into a downward spiral of debt.

Do The Math

"Merchant cash advances and factoring can often be a very expensive way to fund your business", warns Adam Cohen, cofounder and CEO of QuarterSpot, a company that aims to help business owners secure loans that are fairly and transparently priced. "The effective rates for some of those options can be 100% or more," he says. "Furthermore, there may be prepayment penalties which means the business owner cannot refinance out of one of these deals without paying a steep price."

Compare the fees you are paying to the amount you are borrowing, and be sure to take into account the length of time involved. For example, if you get $20,000 as a merchant cash advance and pay a $4000 fee, the 20% fee may not seem so bad. After all, 20% is similar to what a cash advance on your credit card would cost. But if you pay back that amount in 6 months, rather than a year, then you're really paying more like 40%—

and actually even more since the balance is decreasing each time you pay back some of the advance. Ask the merchant cash advance providers you are considering (hopefully you will shop around) to give you a projected Annual Percentage Rate (APR) so you can compare offers.

You now know that there are various types of financing available. To get it you need a solid foundation, which is up next in Part Two.

Part Two: The Foundation For Financing

Overview

We've covered a variety of methods for raising money for your business, and if you have made it to this point your head should be spinning with possibilities.

We covered funding sources first in this book because that's probably the reason you decided to read it. But before you rush out to begin raising money, there are some important steps you need to take to build a business that will be as stable and successful as you hope it will be. These steps build the foundation for your venture and can play a crucial role in helping you secure financing and credit when you need them, while protecting cash flow and the company you've worked so hard to establish.

Why Build Your Business Credit Rating?

In our experience, there are plenty of small business owners who can rattle off their personal credit score the moment you ask. But when you ask them about their corporate credit rating, they draw a blank. Business credit ratings are much more mysterious and confusing to them.

The advantages of a strong corporate credit rating are numerous. Such a rating can:

1. Separate your personal and business credit ratings, thereby helping to protect your personal credit scores from the impact of business debt and credit card activity.

2. Help establish the independence of your business entity to help protect your personal assets from business liabilities that arise.

3. Qualify for credit without having to provide risky personal guarantees.

4. Improve your cash flow because you are able to negotiate more favorable terms with your vendors or suppliers.

5. Build a business asset; a strong business credit rating can be valuable if you later decide to sell.

You've no doubt heard the expression, "The time to repair the roof is when the sun is shining." Similarly, the time to build business credit is before you need it. Because this process takes time, the sooner you start, the better.

Build Business Credit For Long-Term Success

Here's an overview of the step-by-step process of building strong business credit. We'll cover many of these steps in more detail in the following chapters, but this will give you an idea of what will be required:

1. Create the proper business structure.
2. Establish and operate a legitimate business that generates revenue.

3. Understand how business credit agencies operate, and register as needed.

4. Establish credit references with companies that report to the major business credit agencies.

5. Increase use of business credit and manage it properly.

6. Monitor your business and personal credit.

7. Grow your business and expand your available credit.

In the early stages, your personal credit will play a role in the loans you receive. If your business or personal credit ratings aren't strong, don't despair. While you work on building your credit ratings you can look to the other sources of financing we've described in Part One of this book. Just make sure you carve out time to build (or rebuild) your credit. As your business grows and expands its search for capital, you will be glad you did.

Let's find out how to get started...

CHAPTER 11

Create Your Business Structure

Betty and John grew up together in Denver, Colorado. After going away to college they returned home to pursue a business career. They were both excellent cooks and decided to start a catering company. Betty and John decided the best way to conduct the new business was to form a Limited Liability Company. So Betty and John filed Articles of Organization with the Colorado Secretary of State. They didn't use an attorney or consult with an accountant ahead of time, because they wanted to save money. They recalled that an organizational meeting was needed, but kept putting it off, and eventually forgot about holding the meeting altogether.

Betty and John didn't know that an LLC, as a separate legal entity, needed to get a Tax ID number (an EIN – Employer Identification Number) from the IRS. If they had gone to a bank to open an LLC bank account, they would have learned this, as banks will not open entity accounts without an EIN number. Instead, the two just assumed they could use their own personal bank accounts and sort things out later. Monies that Betty and John used to advance the company were paid out of their personal accounts directly to vendors. As things progressed, they tried to keep up by putting the receipts for the checks they had written into a designated cupboard in the kitchen. Six months ago, Betty and John received a letter from the Colorado Secretary of State's office, which requested the payment of the year's upcoming fees. They also received a letter from their resident agent, requesting that they pay the upcoming year's resident agent fees. Betty and John didn't understand what was needed, and both requests wound up in the kitchen cupboard.

Betty recalled hearing that when you received the request from the state, it meant that some sort of annual meeting had to be held. But, she thought to herself, the LLC was just her and John. They spoke every day. What did they possibly have to meet about? At some point during the year, the power company needed a form to be signed to switch service over at their new catering location. Betty signed it, writing "Betty Taylor" (her full name) on the signature line, and sent it back.

Betty and John began operating the catering business. Because they had not taken the step of opening a bank account in the name of the LLC, their first client wrote out a check to Betty Taylor.

Their second client had a problem. Food poisoning at a catered event caused many people to become violently ill. While the fault lay with a supplier of bad lettuce, that didn't matter to the host of the party. Betty and John did not have adequate insurance and were sued. The supplier disappeared and could not be found, much less sued. Soon thereafter, they learned what it means to 'pierce the veil.'

In Colorado, by statute, the veil of limited liability that protects individual members of an LLC can be pierced, or set aside, when members fail to follow certain formalities (the same applies to corporations, too). When members conduct their business as though the LLC doesn't exist, or are so careless in their dealings that proper recognition of a separate entity is ignored, personal liability may attach to each member.

A piercing of the veil of limited liability can be devastating, as it was for John and Betty. The host's attorney had absolutely no problem proving a complete lack of entity formality. The evidence was:

- The LLC Charter has been revoked for failure to file Annual Reports.

- No organization or annual meetings of the members or managers were ever held.

- An EIN was never obtained for the entity from the IRS.

- No LLC bank account was ever opened.

- Payments were made to Betty, not the LLC.

- No LLC tax returns were ever filed.

- In at least one contract, Betty had signed as an individual and not as manager of the LLC.

Betty and John were each held personally liable for the attendee's injuries. All of their work, efforts, and dreams were lost because of their failure to take some very simple protective steps. To prevent the veil of limited liability for your business entity from ever being pierced, you need to develop a "mindset of separateness." You are not the entity. The entity is not you. You will help the entity by serving as a manager or general partner and holding an interest in it. In return, the LLC or LP will help you with limited liability and other protections. This mutually beneficial relationship must have separateness if it is to last.

It is important to build a solid foundation before you start applying for credit. That means making sure your business is structured to be as professional and protected as possible.

For more detailed information on asset protection strategies consider reading Garrett Sutton's other books, *Start Your Own Corporation* and *Run Your Own Corporation*. In this section we will focus on how business entities intersect with business credit. If you're operating as a sole proprietor or as a general partnership, neither of which protect your personal assets, the first step you'll want to take is to set up the right business entity. An entity is a separate legal being chartered by a state government. The term is derived from the Latin word 'ens,' meaning a separate thing. The fact that it is separate from you as an individual is a good thing. It allows not only for asset protection but for the building of a separate credit profile.

The Advantages of the Proper Business Entity

Corporations, limited liability companies (LLCs) and limited partnerships (LPs) are business entities that allow you to:

- **Keep Your Businesses and Personal Assets Separate:** This can protect personal assets such as your home and bank account from claims against the business. This is far superior to using a sole proprietorship or general partnership, which again offer no asset protection.

- **Create Separate Entities for Greater Asset Protection:** Some business owners create more than one corporate entity and segregate assets among different business entities for asset protection. This can lower each asset's exposure to claims.

- **Build Business Credit:** You won't get far using a sole proprietorship for business credit-building purposes. You need a separately chartered and active (meaning all state fees are paid) business entity for this purpose.

- **Enjoy Tax Benefits, Lower Audit Rates, and Make More Money:** Sole proprietorships are audited at a rate five times higher than corporations. There are also many tax benefits to using a corporation, LLC or LP. Many business expenses are easily written off and pre-tax dollars can be used for valuable benefits packages. An Experian study found that incorporated business owners had incomes 35 percent higher than the overall population.

Choosing the Proper Entity

Garrett's book *Start Your Own Corporation,* discusses choosing the right entity in great detail. As such, we will briefly review the choices here.

As mentioned, an entity is a business organized according to state law to limit the liability of the owners. Entities can be corporations, LLCs and LPs. While a sole proprietorship or general partnership provides no protection, entities exist to limit your liability.

CORPORATION

A corporation is a separate legal entity formed by individuals and/or other businesses for the benefit of asset protection, tax savings, and ease of ownership. The owners of a corporation are shareholders, while the managers are known as officers and directors. A Nevada corporation offers the greatest asset protection available, which is discussed in my other books.

S CORPORATION

An S corporation is set up to be taxed as a "flow-through entity." The "S," which refers to an IRS code section, allow the shareholders to be taxed only at the individual level—instead of at both the corporate and individual level, thus avoiding the double taxation of a "C" corporation. The S corporation still provides limited liability protection and is a good entity for many business situations. You may only have 100 shareholders in an S corporation, none of which can be non-resident aliens or corporations.

C CORPORATION

Named after its section in the IRS tax code, a C corporation is taxed at two levels. First, the corporation pays taxes on corporate profits. Then, with any money left over, the corporation may distribute profits to the shareholders, who have to pay taxes on these profits, or dividends. Despite the double taxation, C corporations offer many planning and benefit opportunities.

LIMITED LIABILITY COMPANY

A limited liability company (LLC) is again, like a corporation, a separate legal entity formed for limited liability and asset protection purposes. The owners of an LLC are called members and the management are referred to as managers. LLCs are frequently used for holding real estate and other personal assets as well as for conducting business operations. An LLC can be taxed as a disregarded entity, a partnership, S corporation or C corporation. Work with your advisor to choose which form of taxation is best for you.

LIMITED PARTNERSHIP

Once again formed for limited liability purposes, a limited partnership (LP) is a state chartered entity with an extra re-quirement for complete asset protection. The owners of an LP are known as general and limited partners. The management resides exclusively with the general partner. While the limited partners are limited in their liability, the general partners are personally liable for the LP's activities. This unlimited liability can be resolved by forming a corporation or LLC to be the general partner. As such, we need to form two entities (the LP and a corporation or LLC to be the general partner) for complete limited partnership protection.

PROFESSIONAL ASSOCIATIONS (PA's) OR PROFESSIONAL CORPORATIONS (PC's)

These entities are used by doctors, attorneys, accountants and other licensed professionals. In most states, you must be licensed in that profession to be a member of the corporation, and it does not shield you from malpractice claims. Some states allow for professional LLC entities, as well.

Watch out for advisors who try to push "one size fits all" solutions for new businesses. The entity you choose should balance your needs for asset protection, business credit, ownership structuring, and tax strategy. There are trade-offs associated with every entity strategy—which is why the entity you choose should be based on your business type and goals, not someone else's formula.

Choosing Your Business Name

You cannot use the name of a corporation, LLC or LP that is already in use and registered with the state. If you're going to organize in one state and qualify to do business in another state, the name should be available in both states. A corporate name should not be confused with a trade name or trademark. Just because you can incorporate under the name 'Coca Cola, Inc.' in your home state doesn't mean you could use the name in your trade or business. There is a big company in Atlanta that would put an end to that (and would be well within their rights to do so). So while you may be able to incorporate using one name, you will not automatically be protected in using your corporate name as a trade name, unless you file for trademark protection. For more information on trademarks see Chapter 9 of *Run Your Own Corporation*. We also offer a free report, "Winning With Trademarks." More information can be found in the Resource Section.

Please choose your business name carefully! In our experience there are certain types of names that should be avoided for business credit building purposes. These include names like XXX Holdings, XXX Mortgage, XXX Properties, XXX Real Estate, and the like. (It is not the X's we care about but the words Holdings, Mortgage, Properties and Real Estate.) That industry is considered a high risk industry and with certain types of business credit, you are judged by the company you keep.

Please try not to choose your own name as the name of your business, either, unless you really don't care about growing your business to a point where you can cash out. Paul Newman and Martha Stewart aside, owner named businesses can sound less professional. Which sounds more established: Kevin's Landscaping, or Leisure Landscapes?

And if you do decide to sell the business do you want a new owner potentially dragging your good name through the mud? Take some time to think through your business name and bounce it off some other businesspeople and potential clients. Run it through several search engines. See if someone has already trademarked it by doing a search at uspto.gov, the web site for the U.S. Patent and Trademark Office. You don't want to use a name that someone could (rightfully) demand you stop using because it infringes on their existing trademark. You don't want to be stuck with a name you may later outgrow. A good name with an established reputation and clientele, trademark protection and domain names, is truly a business asset.

Choosing Your State of Incorporation

Nevada and Wyoming are popular for privacy and asset protection benefits. Both states have superior charging order protection for LLCs, and Nevada is the only state (at this writing) which extends such protection to corporate shares. As well, both states have no state income taxes. You can then qualify to do business in your home state, for example, California. The qualification process involves having the Wyoming Secretary of State's office (for example) provide a certificate of good standing for the Wyoming LLC, and then filing with the California Secretary of State for permission for the Wyoming LLC to do business in California. While you won't pay any state taxes in Wyomng (besides an annual $50 filing fee) you will have to pay all of the taxes in California (because you would be doing business there).

It's not an overly complicated process, but it's important to ensure that your entity's limited liability protection will follow you into the states where you actively conduct business. For business credit building purposes, it's essential that you be registered in the state where you are doing business, and that your resident agent be in your state.

Following Corporate Formalities

In order to maintain the limited liability protection afforded corporations, LLCs and LPs, certain minimum ongoing requirements must be met. These are known as corporate formalities and include:

- Filing statements and paying annual fees to the state of incorporation and, if applicable, the state(s) of qualification.
- Maintaining a registered agent in each state.
- Providing corporate notice.
- Keeping corporate minutes on an annual basis.

As in the case of Betty and John, failure to follow these formalities can lead to a piercing of the corporate veil, resulting in personal liability to officers, directors and shareholders. That means that the person suing the company sees that the company has no assets, argues that the company didn't follow the required corporate formalities and shows that the owners of the company should be held personally responsible for the claim. You've spent the time and money to raise the veil of protection, let's not lose it by failing to follow some simple rules.

Filing Statements & Paying Annual Fees

Depending on the state where you incorporate, you may have to file an annual report each year and pay annual fees. If you are using a professional incorporation service, ask if they will keep you up to date on the annual filing requirements. If not, make sure you stay on top of this, and keep your corporate filings up to date.

As an example, a client came to us wanting to build corporate credit. He had incorporated through a do-it-yourself service almost three years ago, but he had never filed annual reports or paid filing fees. He couldn't begin to start building business credit until he brought those filings up to date, which included some serious penalties.

Resident or Registered Agents

Each state requires that a resident (or registered) agent be identified and located in the state of incorporation and any states where business is conducted. The resident agent's job is to accept service of process (i.e., notice of a lawsuit) and other official notices on behalf of the entity. You can be your own registered agent, but if you travel it is not suggested. If you are served when you are away you may never get notice of the lawsuit. As well, some states require you to be open for business from 8 am to 5 pm. You are better off using a reputable service—one that is professional, open during the required hours, appreciates the importance of a lawsuit being served, and will be in business for the long-term. As mentioned, using a resident agent is particularly important if you'll be away from the office for extended periods of time. The last thing you want is a default judgment (where the person suing you wins because you weren't notified of the claim in time). Make sure your service is open to accept the service of process and then promptly notify you of it. More on registered agent services is found in the Resource Section.

Give Corporate Notice

It is important to provide the public with notice that your business is a corporation, LLC or LP. To that end, you'll use Inc., LLC, or LP, for example, on your letterhead as well as on all of your brochures, contracts, checks, cards, and the like. If you are incorporated but sign your contracts as 'Joe Jones' instead of 'Joe Jones, President of XYZ, Inc.' someone could assert they thought they were doing business with you personally (unlimited liability) instead of with a corporation (limited liability). Provide corporate notice wherever you can.

Keeping Corporate Minutes

Most states require that the owners and managers of an entity meet once a year to discuss the affairs of the business. To prove that this required meeting took place, minutes detailing decisions made at the meeting are written and kept with the corporate records.

You should also get in the habit of keeping detailed minutes and resolutions throughout the year. If the business is going to take on new debt, for instance, you should have a resolution authorizing it. Again, if you don't prepare the annual meeting minutes (or follow the other 'corporate formalities') a claimant can pierce the corporate veil and get past the corporation to reach your personal assets. If you are not up to date, there are corporate clean up service providers identified in the Resource Section who can bring you current.

Please know that if you follow the formalities we've just mentioned you will have a much easier time with building business credit. For example, by not paying the annual fees, your entity's charter will be revoked by the state. It is literally impossible to gain business credit with a revoked LLC or corporation. Follow the formalities and prosper.

Now let's look into corporate credit...

Chapter 12

Corporate Credit Agencies

In recent years, there has been a lot of attention in the news media to the topic of personal credit reports and scores. As a result, more people than ever seem to be aware of the need to build, maintain and monitor their credit. But business credit is still very much a mystery—even to those who have had their own businesses for years. In this chapter, we will help you understand how business credit agencies work. In the next chapter, we will explain the steps for building strong business credit.

Types of Business Credit Agencies

Not that long ago, if you wanted to see your personal credit report, you would find the local agency (or agencies) that covered your geographic area and then take the time to go there to get a copy. There were hundreds of agencies across the country that had been formed to serve local geographic areas. However, eventually three major firms (Equifax, Experian and TransUnion) acquired local agencies and now we have three major credit reporting agencies that collect and report information about consumers all over the country.

Similarly, business credit agencies often were developed to collect and share information about businesses in a specific geographic area or industry. While there are corporate credit agencies that collect and report information nationwide, some of these smaller agencies still exist. As a result, there are a lot of different business credit agencies. Here's an overview of the corporate credit industry, but keep in mind there are even more than just those listed here:

Major Commercial Credit Reports: D&B, Experian Small Business, Cortera, Equifax Small Business, and the Small Business Financial Exchange.

Industry Specific Credit Reports: Tarnell Company (plastics); SeaFax (food industry); Lyon Mercantile Group (home furnishings and décor, juvenile, textiles and giftware); Lumberman's (construction in Florida); and CreditRisk Monitor (public companies) are some examples.

As you can imagine, it's difficult for a small business to try to keep track of all of the business credit reporting agencies that may collect and report their credit information. You've got enough on your plate trying to run your business! So don't drive yourself crazy over it. Instead, we suggest you focus your time and energy on the top major commercial credit reporting agencies: D&B, Experian Small Business, Equifax Small Business and Cortera. If there is a specialized agency that serves your particular industry, then check that one as well.

Crucial Differences

While entrepreneurs have had some experience with personal credit reports, the commercial credit agencies are foreign territory for most. So before we delve into them, here are a few differences between personal and business credit reports to keep in mind:

No federal law covers business credit reports. This means there are no specific requirements for the commercial credit agencies with regard to accuracy, disputes, or disclosures. There is no requirement, for example, that they provide a free credit report disclosure each year or investigate mistakes within a certain time frame.

Income can matter. On personal credit reports, income isn't even a factor. But when it comes to business credit, the best business credit ratings may go to companies with large revenues and employees, depending on the agency and the information they collect.

Business credit cards don't always help. Unlike personal credit cards, which are essential to building a strong FICO score, with business credit that's not always the case. Why? Because some business cards don't report to the commercial agencies, or they only report to one or two of them.

Vendor and trade credit is important for business credit. If you have reviewed your personal credit, you may have noticed that your cell phone company, utility companies, and others don't usually report. But for some business credit agencies, vendors of these types that report can be essential to building a strong commercial score.

Payment information can be detailed. Account data that is reported can be much more detailed on business credit reports than on personal credit files. A perfect example: Lenders usually won't report a late payment on your personal credit file unless you pay more than 30 days late. But with business credit, you may see a term called "DBT" or "Days Beyond Term." That's the specific number of days past the due date the account is paid. Always pay by the due date—or earlier if possible.

MAJOR COMMERCIAL CREDIT REPORTS

D&B (DUN & BRADSTREET)

D&B offers a number of different types of small business credit reports that are a combination of vendor and lender reported information, public records and other public information, industry trends, and information supplied to D&B by the business owner. Sources and types of information found in D&B reports are:

- Interviews with business owners and managers
- Trade account and bank transactions reported to D&B
- Bankruptcy filings of the business and Secretary of State office filings
- Newspapers, trade publications and electronic news services

Establishing Business Credit with D&B

Your D&B file will become active with your D-U-N-S® number which you can get for free and upon request. (This number is the D&B "equivalent" of a Social Security number and may be required for certain government contracts.)

There are two ways to proactively build a credit file with D&B:

METHOD 1: Request your free D-U-N-S number, and establish credit relationships with vendors that report to D&B. When this information is reported, it will be added to your file. You will find information for getting a D-U-N-S number at DNB.com.

At their website, you will be prompted to search for your business to see if it is already listed. If it is not, then you will be given instructions to either: a) Establish a D&B Credit File (with the CreditBuilder program, which we will describe below), or b) Get a D-U-N-S® number for free. Choose the second option if you simply want to request your free D-U-N-S number.

You will then be taken through several pages where you're asked to enter information about your company. The info you enter here will be used each time you check the Business Information Report, so remember: Be accurate and consistent! Any request for information that is followed by an asterisk is required. You can enter other non-asterisked info if you want. But remember, the more information you provide, the more D&B can check. Also, D&B makes money by selling lists to other companies. So keep in mind that some of your information may be used for marketing purposes.

One of two things will happen next. You will either get your free D-U-N-S number by email in 30 to 45 business days, or you will get an email stating your request could not be completed. You'll be instructed then to call D&B. At this point, you will be asked questions about your business and encouraged to buy additional programs such as DunsFile, Small Business Starter™, or CreditBuilder™.

METHOD 2: Purchase one of the Dun & Bradstreet Credibility Corp's programs described in the previous paragraph, which will expedite the creation of your file by adding your company information and credit references more quickly than if you established credit the traditional way. Dun & Bradstreet Credibility Corp. is a separate company that was essentially spun off of D&B several years ago. It markets services to small businesses to help them establish and monitor their business credit. These programs offer several levels of service, a variety of prices, and pricing which may change. So visit their website for current information.

Several news articles have included stories from entrepreneurs who felt that sales reps gave them a pretty heavy sales pitch for the program. Some said they were led to believe that they could not build an active credit file without it. Our experience shows otherwise.

These programs can help you expedite the addition of certain credit references that may not already report to your business credit file. Purchasing this program from D&B does not ensure you will get a strong Paydex® score, however. If you supply D&B with information that places your business in the high-risk category, or if you have no credit references to report, you will not build your business credit profile just by using this program.

EXPERIAN SMALL BUSINESS

Experian provides business credit reports for approximately 27 million companies in the U.S., including Puerto Rico and the Virgin Islands, and reports the following information:

- Business background information
- Bank, trade, and financial information
- Liens, judgments, and bankruptcies
- UCC filings
- Credit ranking score

"We have coverage in virtually all businesses in the U.S.," says Brian Ward, senior director, Experian Business Information Services. "If you are a small business, chances are Experian has a business credit report on your organization."

Experian has an established track record as a leading provider of consumer credit reports. It was the first reporting agency to offer consumers a plain-English credit report, as well as free annual credit reports before the law required it. Experian brings that experience and positive innovations to the small business credit reporting arena as well.

Because Experian also collects personal credit data, it can create a "blended score" that includes information about the owner's personal credit along with the business's information. Experian is quick to point out, though, that consumer credit report information is highly regulated and will not be provided to just anyone. Businesses who want to obtain a blended score must have the written permission of the person whose information will be accessed, or a permissible purpose under the federal Fair Credit Reporting Act.

Establishing Business Credit with Experian

You do not establish a file directly with Experian, because it does not take "self-reported information," but instead relies on information from third party sources. Once a company that reports to Experian supplies information about your account, Experian will establish your file. Your file will then be tracked by company name, address, and an Experian-created Business Identification Number (B.I.N.). If your company is someday sold, merges with another company, or you change the name, you may want to notify Experian to make sure its records are updated as well.

Experian offers several different types of business credit reports, including an annual subscription with credit monitoring. You can learn more about those products on their website.

CORTERA (formerly eCredit)

Cortera tracks $1.6 trillion in business purchases across 45 spend categories to deliver insights on 20 million U.S. businesses. One thing that sets it apart is the affordability of its reports.

Cortera offers reports for as little as $3 per report, or they offer inexpensive subscriptions that allow companies to monitor their customers. One service, for example, allows a business to monitor all of their customers at a price that is cheaper than a single commercial report with some other services.

Information in Cortera reports may include:

Spending behavior (spending in materials, operations and shipping over the last 12 months)

Payment behavior (how the company has paid over the last 6 months) or payment behavior within a certain industry

Community payment reviews

Recent news

Executives

Competitors

Demographics

Public records

Establishing Business Credit With Cortera

You can find out if your company is listed in Cortera's database for free. Simply go to the website: www.Cortera.com and enter your company's name. If your business is not found, you will be given the opportunity to supply basic information that will be used to establish your credit profile.

Note: If you operate your business from your home, it may not be included in Cortera's database. The company does not list home business addresses for security reasons. In addition, if your business operates from a PO Box or similar type of address, it will not likely be included in the Cortera database. Your business should have a physical, non-home-based address to be listed. Exceptions are made on a case-by-case basis.

SMALL BUSINESS FINANCIAL EXCHANGE

In 2001, a group of 175 lenders (including all the big names you would recognize like Bank of America, American Express, etc.) joined together to create a non-profit credit reporting agency —the Small Business Financial Exchange. The SBFE states that is it not a business credit agency and does not compile business credit reports. Instead, it calls itself a data exchange. Members share information about their customers and, in turn have access to information from other members that can be used for credit purposes. That data cannot, however, be used for marketing purposes. Currently the SBFE has information on some 24 million small businesses, which it defines as businesses with less than $10 million in revenue and less than $2.5 million in loan exposure with the financial institution reporting.

Another key difference from some other agencies is that it does not contain any self-reported data. In other words, business owners cannot report information that will be included in these reports.

The types of information reported by SBFE is very specific and only includes member reported information about lines of credit, loans, credit cards, leases, and SBA loans. Other information reported includes business name and address, account type and status, date opened, credit limit and high credit, and payment history. (It reports both positive and negative information about payment history.) The information in the report can be used to create credit scores by the SBFE or each individual member can create its own credit scores.

Establishing Business Credit With SBFE

When an SBFE member (a lender) reports information about your account, it will be part of the information available to other

SBFE members. Companies are tracked using the company name and Employer Identification Number (EIN).

The SBFE does not currently offer the opportunity to order its report on your small business directly from them. Instead you must request your report from one of their authorized vendors, and currently Equifax is the only company authorized to do so.

EQUIFAX COMMERCIAL INFORMATION SOLUTIONS

Equifax Commercial Information Solutions offers several types of reports about small businesses: Small Business Credit Report, Small Business Credit Monitoring, Business Risk Indicator Report, and Business Risk Monitoring.

Equifax obtains information from the SBFE that includes loan, lines of credit and lease data; information from vendors that offer businesses that offer products and services on a net 30 invoice basis; as well as public record and publicly available information. These files contain no "self-reported" information. Equifax uses a unique 9-digit identifier called EFX ID to track a business's credit history.

Establishing Business Credit with Equifax

You do not establish a commercial credit file directly with Equifax. If a vendor or lender reports information or inquires about your business, your file will be created. You can purchase your credit report on the Equifax Small Business website.

What's Your Small Business Score?

FICO SBSS (Small Business Scoring Service) models are used to help underwrite certain types of small business loans, including some SBA and Export-Import Bank guaranteed loans.

One of these scores, the FICO's SBSS score draws in personal credit, business credit and financial data, and uses it to produce a score. It may be used for new loans as well as to evaluate or "rescore" existing loan portfolios.

The range for this score is 0 - 300, with the higher number being "better" in that it represents less risk to the lender.

NAV

Until recently, however, business owners have not generally had access to these scores. Nav is a company that is changing that by offering products that allow business owners to monitor both their personal and business credit scores. Just as it's a good idea to check your personal credit before you apply for an important loan like a mortgage, it's a good idea to check these scores before you apply for a small business loan. In addition, ongoing monitoring can alert you to problems—including business identity theft, which is a fast-growing and serious crime.

In addition, when you establish a free account with Nav you'll have access to a wealth of credit-building information. For information on how to use this service to your advantage, and special offers on premium services visit our Resource Section.

Fixing Mistakes On Your Business Credit Reports

We've warned you a couple of times that when mistakes appear on your credit report, they may be difficult to correct. We emphasize that because we don't want you to be careless about how you build your commercial credit files. It's a legitimate warning, based on our experience with business owners over the years.

But don't assume the worst if you do discover your business credit file contains wrong data. Dispute the mistakes, keep good records of your dispute (including copies of any corre-spondence), and keep a positive mindset going into the process. Hopefully, your mistakes will be cleared without a hitch!

Each commercial credit reporting agency publishes infor-mation on how to dispute a mistake. In some cases, you may not be able to get information reported by a third party corrected, but you can add a statement to your file explaining your side of the story. In the case of SBFE data, you will currently need to contact Equifax to dispute the contents of any report.

In the next chapter, we will walk you through the overall process of building strong business credit...

Chapter 13

Steps for Building Business Credit

Your personal credit reports are created when you first establish credit with a lender that reports to one or more of the three major credit reporting agencies. The process of building business credit is somewhat similar to that process. When you get credit with a lender which then reports to one or more commercial credit agencies you can get started.

But there's a twist: you don't have to have a business credit card, loan or line of credit in order to establish a business credit report with some of these agencies. That's because they may gather information from a wider variety of sources than are used in personal credit. As a result, when you go to check your credit with the agencies listed in the previous chapter, you may find that your company is already listed in their database, even if you have few or no credit accounts reporting. So how do you build business credit?

Step 1: Building A Foundation for Business Credit

The following are steps we recommend you follow when building corporate credit. Some may be directly related to this process, while others may be helpful in the overall process of establishing your venture for funding.

Check your personal credit scores(s). If there is more than one principal in the business, each of them should check their scores. If your scores are high, you are likely to get approved very easily. If not, consult Garrett's 2012 edition of *The ABC's of Getting Out of Debt* for strategies on building better credit.

You can check your credit reports for free once a year at AnnualCreditReport.com. In addition, Credit.com's free service offers two free credit scores from one of the major credit reporting agencies, updated once a month. And Nav currently offers business owners a free personal report summary from one of the major credit reporting agencies. Checking your credit yourself does not hurt your credit rating. As a business owner, you should definitely stay on top of your personal credit reports and scores.

Properly form your business. As explained previously, you must establish the proper business structure, whether it's a Corporation (S Corp or C Corp), LLC, or LP. Set up the right business entity at the start. We can't emphasize that enough. The benefits extend far beyond establishing business credit.

Keep your date of incorporation and articles of incorporation or organization handy. When you are asked for that date, make sure you accurately report it. Some will want proof of your entity, which a copy of the Articles provides. Also, be sure to speak to your accountant before filling out this form to find out whether your business should operate on a fiscal year or calendar year basis. This can be important, depending on the nature and seasonality of your business.

Keep current on your filings. If you're incorporated, your articles of incorporation should be filed with your state, and all corporate filing fees should be paid. If you incorporated in another state, such as Nevada or Wyoming, find out if you need to register as a "foreign" corporation in the state where your company is actually located, and take the steps required to make sure your business is fully recognized in its state of operation. It's very difficult for out-of-state Wyoming or Nevada corporations to build business credit without a physical address in the state where they are doing business.

Get an Employer Identification Number (EIN). You must get an EIN when you incorporate your business. If you don't already have one, you can get one from the IRS website. Go to IRS.gov and find Form SS4 to fill out. Your EIN will be on all tax filings and is required to open a business bank account.

Choose your industry code. The Standard Industrial Classification (SIC) and North American Industry Classification System (NAICS) codes were created for statistical tracking purposes. They describe the primary activity of the business. Their use goes far beyond those purposes, though. For example, the official Census website explains that some state governments offer tax incentives to businesses classified in specified NAICS industries. Some contracting authorities require businesses to register their NAICS codes, which are used to determine eligibility to bid on certain contracts.

In 1997, NAICS codes replaced SIC codes for statistical purposes since they are more detailed. You can learn about SIC and NAICS codes on the Census.gov website.

Choose this code carefully. The SIC and NAICS code can influence your business credit scores because your venture may be compared with others in the same industry, depending on which type of report is used. If the businesses in the NAICS code you choose have a track record of paying bills late or failing, your scores may be affected, even if your company is doing fine. You must be truthful, but if your business has more than one focus, you may want to carefully consider which category to choose for your businesses' SIC or NAICS code. For example, some real estate investors (which alone is a risky niche) also engage in marketing and management, and decide to focus on those activities when choosing their industry codes. One of Garrett's clients had an experience with this firsthand. She explains, "Banks do not want to see the category of REIT (real estate investment) or the SIC code of 6798. They are more comfortable if you are categorized as real estate consulting and management as opposed to real estate investing. I was able to get my SIC updated to 8742 as my husband and I do property management and he consults on commercial construction deals. The key thing with changing my SIC code was that your credit ranking classes change and now I am showing as a low risk versus moderate risk when I was listed as a REIT."

Get a business checking account. You must establish a checking account in the name of your business, and use it for business purposes only. You should do this as soon as possible after you incorporate. Make sure your business name and information is listed on your application exactly as you want it to appear from now on. In other words, make sure your EIN is accurate, the name of the business is spelled out completely and exactly the way it officially appears in your corporate records, the address is completely correct and the like. It will be much more difficult to straighten this out later.

Do not intermingle business and personal funds. You may lose valuable tax deductions, or even put the legitimacy of your corporation at risk. You may get some "credit," so to speak, by keeping an average balance in your account of at least $5,000 to $10,000 each month. This helps demonstrate stability on the part of the business.

If you can't deposit at least a few grand in the account, try to show higher month-end or average daily balances. That may mean paying your bills at the beginning of the month, and doing your best to get paid and to deposit that money into your account by the end of the month. Don't make late payments on bills, though, or you'll wipe out the benefit of a larger bank account.

The longer your business bank account has been established, the better in certain cases. So choose your banking relationship carefully. It's one you'll want to stick with for a good, long time. Ideally, you'll want this account to be at least six months old before you apply for credit.

Don't bounce checks! If you have been lazy about balancing the checkbook before, you cannot afford to let it slide anymore. You must stay on top of your balances to avoid "Non-Sufficient Funds" (or NSF) notices. You don't need to be taking two steps backwards here.

Be smart about your business location. The business credit system can be somewhat stacked against home-based businesses. A P. O. Box location or executive office suite can also be a problem, although some business owners have successfully established their credit using boxes at UPS Stores or similar locations, where they can be identified with a street number and individual box number. We recommend using your home over one of these locations, as vendors and banks like to have a physical address where they can collect any collateral or serve legal documents in the event of a default.

Ideally, you'll want a physical business location separate from any other business. But that doesn't mean you have to go

out and lease an office if it doesn't make sense. If you do operate from home, or sublease space from another business, make
sure you at least get the proper occupational licenses. If yours
is a foreign corporation, you should have a location in your
home state, separate from your resident agent, for credit-building
purposes.

Get a business phone number. You must have a business
phone number that is listed with 411 directory assistance under
your company's name. Not that long ago, the only way to
do that was to pay for a business phone line from your local
telecom. Now you can use *ListYourself.net* to submit your cell
phone number, VOIP phone, or even a virtual answering service,
to 411 directories. You can create a local listing for free, and regional or national listings for a fee. It can take a while for your
listing through this service to appear in some 411 directories,
so list your business as soon as possible.

Find out what licenses you need. You must get the proper
occupational licenses for your business, even if you work from
your home. Do this as soon as you establish your business
checking account and form your corporate identity. If you rent
or lease a property, check to make sure it's OK to run your
business from that location. You can usually get information
on business license requirements in your area from your local
or regional Small Business Development Center.

Keep a copy of your business license with your corporate
papers. You may be required to provide these as proof of your
self-employment for certain types of loans. Be consistent! Use
the same information each time you apply for credit. Don't use
"Suite 122" one time and "#122" another. Keep dates consistent and accurate, and use careful, clear handwriting!

One of our clients discovered a problem with her D&B file. She has been following our advice for building business credit but D&B showed no record of a file. She investigated, and found out that some of her vendors had misspelled her company's name. She got them to correct the mistakes, then she went to D&B, and they made the correction as well. It took some time, but she finally got everything straightened out. Since more than one vendor misspelled the company name, it's possible she either entered it inconsistently, or her handwriting wasn't clear.

Step 2: Start Building References

Get a Business Credit Card. As we discussed in Chapter 2, you may want to get a business credit card to use for your business instead of using a personal credit card. A business credit card is not required in order to build a positive credit rating, but it can be helpful, at least with regard to some of the corporate credit agencies. As we discussed, these cards have their pros and cons.

ADVANTAGES:

A business credit card:

- Can be fairly easy to qualify for if you have good personal credit
- Can simplify record-keeping
- Can offer fees and interest that are often tax deductible if not mingled with personal use
- May not report to personal credit agencies, so they won't affect your personal credit reports, except if you default

DISADVANTAGES

A business credit card can also:

- Almost always require a personal guarantee

- Usually result in an inquiry into your personal credit

- Not report to all business credit agencies

- Not always carry the same consumer protections available on personal credit cards

Request your free D-U-N-S® number. This is the D&B equivalent of a Social Security number for your business. Only when you have completed the steps above is it time to request your D-U-N-S number. In the previous chapter we explained a couple of options for ways to get your free D-U-N-S number and to begin establishing your credit history with D&B.

Establish one or two initial trade references. After you have completed the steps above you can get your first trade accounts. You want to work with vendors that report to at least one major business credit agency. Apply for one at a time and make sure you use your EIN and businesses name, not your Social Security number when you apply. Use them, and pay everything on time. Many companies will extend business credit, but, unfortunately for credit building, few report.

Keep building strong credit references. Once the groundwork is laid, you'll want to start adding additional credit references. Whenever possible, work with vendors or lenders willing to report your on-time payment or purchase history to one or more business credit agencies, and avoid those that will report your accounts on your personal credit reports.

Keep in mind that many lenders will report *defaults* on business credit cards to the *personal* credit reporting agencies. So no matter what, if you can't pay one of these accounts back, your personal credit will be damaged. However, if you pay on time, then most of these cards won't affect your personal credit at all. And that's a good thing, because you want to keep your business and personal credit separate as much as possible.

Don't apply for too many accounts in a short period of time, as those inquiries may affect your personal credit if those lenders review personal credit. Your goal, however, should be to have five or six accounts that report to and major business credit reporting agencies. Use the accounts actively, always paying before the due date. You'll want to continue to expand your credit and the amount of credit available to your business. Your initial limits will be low, but they should increase with each additional vendor.

Step 3: Ongoing Business Credit Once you have completed the steps above, you will not only begin to establish credit, but you will also begin separating your business credit from your personal credit. Your personal credit scores won't be challenged. It can't be emphasized enough that growing businesses can run into huge financial roadblocks if owners are only relying on their personal credit. At some point banks and other lenders say no. By building business credit and separating it from your personal credit you have a second track of credit for lenders to review and accept. In time, most vendors will rely on a business credit application and qualification, without even looking at your personal credit. Again, whenever possible, you'll select vendors who report to the business credit agencies. By doing business with them, and paying on time, you can start building a positive business credit score. You can start developing that second track of credit for your future growth. There are more steps that are recommended if you want to build a successful business. Though they may not necessarily be required to build business credit, they can help position yourself for longer term success:

Hire a tax pro. Even if you want to do your own book-keeping, it's a good idea to also establish a relationship with a tax attorney or an accountant, preferably a CPA, who has experience working with small businesses. You'll likely need the accountant's help to generate financial statements, as well as to make sure you are handling payroll and other tax details correctly.

If you are applying for a mortgage as a self-employed bor-rower, you may need to ask your CPA or tax professional for a letter stating that you have been self-employed for the required number of years (usually two). This is another good reason to work with a tax professional.

Hire a bookkeeping or payroll service. If you'll be an employee or you will have employees, get a bookkeeping or payroll service to administer your payroll. Mistakes are easily made in this area and the IRS does not have a sense of humor about them (as evidenced by the criminal penalties that can arise.) Garrett's book, *Run Your Own Corporation*, discusses these important issues in greater detail. For referrals to a nation-al bookkeeping service see the Resource Section.

Set up a business website and email address. If you're seri-ous about your business, we strongly recommend you set up a business website—even if it's just a page—and get an email address that is "branded" to your company. For example, if your company is named XYZ Inc., then you'd want an email address like info@xyzinc.com. It is inexpensive to do this, and well worth it. Skip generic email addresses like xyzinc@gmail.com or xyzinc@hotmail.com. They just don't look professional anymore. Websites are the new business card. And when you hand out your business card, your website should be listed on it.

Develop a two-year track record. A two-year track record is very helpful, as some credit applications will require you to have been in business for at least this long before offering terms or business credit. If you previously operated the business as a sole proprietorship and have the tax records to back that up, then you should be able to use that information as the date you started the business. But keep in mind that if dates don't match, your business may be labeled as high risk.

Please also know that promoters selling two year old companies with 'established' lines of business credit may be selling you an illusion. When you take over the company those lines of credit most often evaporate (if they truly existed at all). You don't 'buy' business credit. You build it.

Stay away from those who would tell you otherwise.

Step 4: Dealing with Rejection

As an entrepreneur, you need thick skin. Rejection of all kinds is just part of the deal. But when you do get rejected for credit, you should take three important steps:

Find out why you were turned down. If the letter you get doesn't explain why you were rejected, or you don't understand the reasons, give the company a call. Ask to speak to someone in the credit department, and see if you can get more info about why you weren't approved. At large companies, this may be harder than in smaller companies, but it's worth a try.

Order your credit report. If the company used your *personal* credit as part of the evaluation, they are required by law to tell you how to request a free copy. Take advantage of this opportunity to get your credit report. (Keep a copy for your records.) If a commercial credit report was used, you may also be instructed that you can get a free copy of this report. Again, if that is the case, take advantage of this chance to see what your file contains.

Ask to be reconsidered. If you believe the reasons why you were rejected aren't accurate, or if you can supply additional information, it doesn't hurt to ask to be reconsidered. Smaller lenders or vendors in particular want your business, and you may be able find someone on staff who is willing to work with you. If the answer is still "no," see whether they are willing to share with you what steps you need to take to get a "yes."

You didn't get where you are by accepting lame or non-sensical responses. While you have to be cordial, you will also assert your position. Business credit is not some sugar coated plum only a few lucky people get to have. Rather, it is earned using the steps we have discussed here. You build towards it. If you have followed these steps you should obtain it. Assert yourself and do so.

Now you are ready for the next phase of financing...

Part Three:
Financing with Equity

Overview

Now that we have covered the many traditional ways to raise money for your business and build up its business credit it is time to move into prime time. You are ready for it.

In Parts One and Two we've learned the financing strategies to get your business off the ground and into a stable business credit setting. In Part Three we are going to discuss bringing investors into the company. Not the sympathetic Mom and Dad kind of investors—those who love you anyway—but rather the hard-nosed, serious investors who expect quite a lot. The investors who will only give a small measure of love after a gigantic windfall in their favor. Yes, you are ready for these types.

The laws we are going to cover apply to every type of investor—hard-nosed or sympathetic. The securities laws, as they are called, are known to sophisticated investors. They know that you have to discuss risk factors (problems the company may face in the future) and that you can't make promises as to performance (otherwise you may be held to those promises).

Your friends and family may be just as likely to not understand the requirements of the securities laws. They will ask: Why are you scaring potential investors away by overly drawing attention to all these risks? And why aren't you writing about how well you are going to do for everyone?

Because you can't, you will tell them. The securities laws say not to, and you'll get in trouble if you do. If they need to know more, you may simply suggest that they also read this section.

The securities laws are very strict about disclosure. You've got to allow a potential investor to make an informed decision. So you've got to tell them everything—the good, the bad and the ugly.

You will tell them up front what the risks are of investing in the company. As well, you can't get their hopes up by making wild promises about glorious returns. That may never happen, and you know it.

So you'll tell them the truth; that you will do your best but can make no guarantees. In this light the securities laws make sense: A federal requirement to give people the information they need to make a reasoned decision.

Over time, however, the securities laws got so restrictive that they prevented the formation of capital. For an economy to grow and succeed, new companies need to be able to acquire new monies to pursue new opportunities. When the securities laws severely restrict the flow of information on such opportunities the result is that capital formation and job creation suffer.

To alleviate the problem, Congress passed the JOBS Act in the spring of 2012. The intent is to open up the securities laws to allow for greater investment in new and development phase companies. We shall discuss this further in Chapter 15 on Crowdfunding.

With the advent and implementation of these new securities laws, many more companies will be financing with equity. That is, they will be bringing money into the company by selling stock (or shares) in the company.

You may find yourself in a position to invest in one of these companies. What lies ahead will help you as both a business owner raising money for your company and as well as an investor looking into opportunities with other companies.

Please know that this next section can get pretty technical. If you aren't quite ready for bringing in investors consider jumping ahead to Section Four, where we have some very helpful information for all business owners.

If you are forging ahead, let's start with the professional investors...

Chapter 14

Angels and Venture Capital

Julia Pimsleur comes from a family known for its successful foreign language teaching systems. When creating her own method for children to learn a language, she had to learn to develop and market a product and run a business from scratch —including how to raise capital.

A mother herself, she wanted to create an affordable and high-quality program for teaching children how to speak a foreign language, and knew she could do better than what was presently available on the market. She also realized there was a market opportunity in creating a product for very young children, an underserved market. So she set about creating a lovable panda character named Little Pim who would appeal to very young children and designed the Entertainment Immersion Method®, the first method ever to help kids up to age 6 learn a language at the age they learn best.

She had a background in film, so her first step was to produce a five minute pilot video that she financed herself. A friend from college was the first to invest, and from there Julia raised about half a million dollars in angel funding to develop the first three DVDs in her series. She sold DVDs off a simple website she created…and kept her day job. The next year she was able to raise $1 million to launch the company with a small staff—including herself—and add in a marketing budget.

"I learned the importance of bringing people into your vision early on," she says. "Put your wish out there with numbers behind it to people who can help." She made it a point to talk with anyone who might be able to help her grow her business, or provide a connection to someone who could.

Little Pim has gone on to win 25 awards, get national distribution in Barnes and Noble and Toys "R" Us and has been featured in national and regional news stories, including on The Today Show and The View. Most importantly, parents are buying the DVDs and digital downloads of the same series (over 2 million sold to date) and sharing their testimonials of how the program helped their children on the company's website at LittlePim.com.

As the author of the book *Million Dollar Women*, about women entrepreneurs who have created multimillion dollar companies, Julia shares three lessons with other entrepreneurs trying to raise money:

1. Take Risks. "Women sometimes have a tendency to play it safe, but to raise money you need to embrace the risk involved and move forward despite the fear. No one can know for sure whether their business will be a success," she says. "I may not have all the answers but I know not to be intimidated about that." Men can benefit from that advice, too!

2. Know your numbers. "You should have a firm grasp of the key parts of your company's finances," she insists. "It wasn't the part I loved best but getting comfortable with talking about margins, COGs and EBIDTA has helped me tremendously."

3. Treat investors as partners. In her first two years in business, Julia sent her investors full 10-page reports

each quarter. "Keep people interested and informed and they may become bigger investors," she says.

Angels and VCs

Angel investors and venture capitalists (VCs) both provide early funding. The similarities end there. VCs, being nicknamed "vulture capitalists," are some tough birds. They have to be. They take on risks where even angels fear to tread.

Three friends were meeting in a coffee house frequented by entrepreneurs and investors. Aubrey had made some money on two difficult but rewarding startups and was now looking to invest her own money into new companies run by others. Victor was a hard charging venture capitalist with a large VC firm. Edgar was an entrepreneur working on a new startup.

"I like what I see," said Victor, the VC, starting right in. "We can begin the due diligence process next month to fully investigate the feasibility."

"And that takes how long?" said Edgar.

Victor replied, "At least six months. We've got to check everything out."

"Our angels can decide in two meetings," said Aubrey.

"That's more like it!" said Edgar. "We've got to be ahead of the market. Waiting six months doesn't work for our plan."

"But we can bring the money you need to the table," said Victor. "I see you needing at least $3 million to fund this."

"No, $3 million builds the company," said Aubrey. "That's for later. You need $300,000 to build the product. And you need to do that now. Our angels clearly see that."

"Well, we don't do such small amounts," said Victor. "It costs us almost that much to do our due diligence research on you."

"If I went with your VC firm," Edgar asked, "what else would you need?"

Victor said, "A seat on the board of directors and control over future funding rounds. We will have several industry experts working alongside your management. It is all detailed in our 90 page deal memorandum."

Aubrey smiled, "Is that all?"

Edgar laughed. "What do angels need?"

"A few hours of your time. We don't want a seat on your board and we're not going to put experts into your company. We don't want to build a company. Let the VCs do that later. We just want to prove that the product is viable."

Edgar said, "And the legal documents…"

"Are a few pages," said Aubrey quickly. "There is nothing complex about this."

"Yes there is," said Victor.

"Not really," said Aubrey. "We'll get Edgar what he really needs, a reasonable amount of money to prove up the product. We take no seat on the board, don't require control of later rounds and don't build companies like you VCs do. We just get the idea off the ground."

"I get it," said Edgar. "We'll start with Aubrey's angels. When the product takes hold, we'll build the company with Victor's VCs. Thanks."

And that briefly identifies the basic differences between angels and VCs. Small investments vs. large amounts of capital. Quick decisions vs. lengthy due diligence. Hands off approach vs. board seats and control. Simple terms vs. complex legal documents.

Each has their place in the economic ecosystem. If your product is proven, angels may not be the right choice as they aren't as well funded or experienced (or even interested) in building strong company platforms. And know that you can have angels participating in VC rounds and VCs acting as angels in early rounds. Just be careful that the VC in the angel round doesn't act like a VC. When you want flexibility and they are headed towards formality, control problems can arise.

It has been reported that it took only $1 million to come up with Facebook's operating system. It took many millions more to build the company, its systems and its talent pool. Angels can give a product life. VCs are the Seabees, akin to the U.S. Navy Construction Battalion (CBs or Seabees) they build whole enterprise infrastructures on the fly while under fire. It can be useful to have both teams on your side.

Investigation Process

Both angels and VCs will investigate a potential candidate for funding the process. Known as due diligence, this can be cursory or comprehensive depending on the firm. A due diligence checklist of items to be considered is found in Appendix A.

The process for both types of investors is generally the same:

- Business Plan. The investor reviews the company's business plan and speaks with the company's founders or officers if the investor's criteria are met. Many funds focus on specific industries, geographic regions and/or stages of development (seed, expansion, etc.).

- Due Diligence. If interest exists, the investor will look into great detail the company's products and services, operating history, management team, financials and other criteria discussed below.

- Term Sheet. If after due diligence the investor is still interested a term sheet describing the terms and conditions under which the investor would invest is prepared.

- Investment and Execution. The monies are invested and the VC investor becomes actively involved in the company. As noted, an angel investor may take a less active role.

- Exit. Both VCs and angels expect to 'exit' the company at some point. While time horizons may vary this is generally between three to ten years after the initial investment. Exits occur through mergers or acquisitions by larger companies or IPOs (Initial Public Offerings) whereby company stock is sold to the public while investors cash out.

Investment Criteria

Each angel group and VC firm will have their own set of requirements which they will, in some cases, make publicly available. As an example, the following serves as the criteria for a regional angel group. (The word 'we' refers to their specific standards.)

While the merits of each investment will vary, we evaluate your venture according to the following criteria:

- Management team. We look for teams of high-quality entrepreneurs with a track record of leadership and performance—either in the company's specific industry or in prior entrepreneurial ventures. We also look at your team's passion for and commitment to the new business idea, and your ability to inspire confidence among future stakeholders, including employees, potential customers, and investors. As we will be working together as partners, your team's credibility is essential. In addition, your team must be open to and comfortable with receiving input provided by angel investors.

- Market opportunity. We invest in solutions that address major problems for significantly large target markets (i.e. a $100+ million market). Your company must demonstrate a strategy to claim significant share of this market (i.e. 20%+). There are plenty of great business ideas—but not all businesses will generate returns that justify angel investor and venture capital financing. Therefore, providing a solution to a problem with a large potential market is essential.

- Use of proceeds. Funds must be used to accelerate your company's achievement of key milestones that increase the company's value. We often fund activities that include research and product development, building a sales and marketing infrastructure and hiring key executives.

- Growth potential. We look for companies that can grow quickly and manage the scale necessary to succeed. Your company must demonstrate a plan to generate significant profits beyond the initial product idea. Do you have a strategy to achieve multiple sources of revenue? We will also require well-conceived financial projections, based on sound assumptions, demonstrating consistent profits and cash flow growth.

- Competitive advantage. Your company must have some proprietary features that distinguish you from potential competitors or provide barriers to entry that prevent other companies from capturing your customers with a similar offering. Attributes that convey competitive advantage include intellectual property protection, exclusive licenses, exclusive marketing and distribution relationships, strong brands, scarce human resources (i.e. knowledge and skills), and access to scarce raw materials.

- Fit. Our group members—all accredited individual investors—have significant executive experience in a variety of fields. One of the benefits of working with angel investors is the active coaching and contact network that such investors can provide. As such, there must be a fit between members of our group and your idea.

- Technology. We prefer to invest in first-of-a-kind new ideas, rather than incremental enhancements to common products and services. Is this a nice-to-have, or a need-to-have product or service? However, we approach highly complex, esoteric technologies with caution. The concept behind the technology must be proven and verifiable. Further, we avoid science projects that don't demonstrate a clear path to commercialization. Any breakthrough innovation must be accompanied by a strong business plan.

- Exit strategy. Our members typically seek returns of at least ten times their initial investment, within eight years. This level of return on investment is essential due to the high risk and likelihood of failure among early stage ventures. Thus, a clearly articulated exit strategy—how angel investors will extract such returns—is essential. For example, do you plan to sell the company to an established corporation in your industry? Or will your exit be through subsequent rounds of financing—venture capital or the public markets? Angel investors are not just interested in the strategy you select, but more importantly in the how—the operational strategy that shows specific steps you will take to achieve the exit.

Common mistakes

Both angels and VCs find that entrepreneurs consistently make the same mistakes. Knowing this, it is important to understand what to avoid.

- Failing to clearly identify the opportunity

As the old saying goes: "Don't hide your light under a bushel." Don't be afraid to show your talents or accomplishments, or in this case, the opportunity your business plan presents. If you are going to rock the industry, say so, and back it up with a clear narrative based on reliable sources and projections. If you are going to fill a niche no one has exploited say so and, again, back it up.

You may know the opportunity like the back of your hand. But investors are coming in cold. They know nothing, much less the back of any body part. The more clearly you can identify, the more you grab them right up front with your excellent prospects, the better chance you have at getting funded.

- Unrealistic projections and simplistic assumptions

Will your business grow at a 50% pace for the next decade? Well, potentially it could. But it is not likely, and investors will close the money vault if your plan is unrealistic.

Work with your team to ensure that your projections (think revenues and profits) and your assumptions (think cost of goods and profit margins) are sound and achievable. Be ready to defend your numbers as existing in the real world.

- A lack of competitive information

Angels and VCs want to know who you are going to crush and how you are going to crush them. They want to know you have done a thorough job of market research and competitive analysis. And they want you to clearly present a coherent case for why your product or service will be superior.

- Failing to line up a strong management team

As another old saying goes: "Money follows management." For angels and/or VCs to be interested you must have an experienced management team made up of people who have been previously successful. Some stress that the lack of a strong management team is the number one reason VCs decline to invest. Don't make this mistake with your plan.

- Spelling, grammar and math mistakes

Never send a first draft of your business plan out to an investor. Instead, you and your team must comb through it for spelling errors, typos, grammar glitches, math mistakes and the like. If you are too close to it all, hire a proofreader. Then have your mentor, mom and dad and as many trusted others as possible critique it for clarity and comprehension.

The importance of a well drafted business plan cannot be overstated. For more information on this important topic, please see *Writing Winning Business Plans* by Garrett Sutton.

Some people, however, need just a jolt to get interested.

The Pitch Deck

A pitch deck is a short presentation providing a quick overview of your business. In essence, you are pitching your opportunity using a deck of slides. As investors—and all of us— have shorter attention spans, a brief, compelling and visually attractive presentation can move people from apathy towards engagement.

Whether you use PowerPoint, Prezi or Keynote to create slides, your pitch must not have too many of them. A basic pitch deck will feature only a dozen or so slides, and only one slide for each key point. All of the slides should be consistent in size, color, font and format. They should draw the investor in. If you don't have the right skill set within your team, a graphic designer can be hired on a project basis to assist.

Consider the following pitch deck presentation:

1. Introduction
Who are you and what is your idea?

2. Team
Who will carry it forward?

3. Problem
What are you solving?

4. Uniqueness
How can you uniquely solve it?

5. Solution
Describe your solution

6. Product or Service
Show examples of how you deliver the solution

7. Market
How big is your target market?

8. Revenue model
How does the money come in?

9. Competition
Who is out there and how will you compete against them?

10. Growth Strategies
How will you roll it out and grow the business?

11. Investment
How much do you need? Be sure to ask for it.

12. Contact
Where can they reach you?

Obviously, you are not going to discuss every facet of your business in just 12 slides. With a pitch deck it is acceptable to leave some material out. The idea is to generate interest so that investors will ask more questions later.

As with any presentation, the more you practice in front of friends and family willing to offer an honest, constructive critique, the better. Know that if you lose people early on it is very hard to get them back. So you will improve and refine your presentation until you are ready to engage and impress your audience. Examples of successful pitch decks can be found on numerous websites, including pitchenvy.com.

Does a pitch deck replace a business plan? No. A business plan forces you to flesh out all of the issues. It forces you to think about all the questions an investor may ask. To get to 12 basic high points for a pitch deck you have to build upon the solid foundation of a well thought out and comprehensive business plan. As well, some investors will want to see your business plan after viewing the pitch deck. Since you want no potholes on the road to financing success, it is best to have that business plan in hand ready to smoothe the way.

Will your personal credit be an issue?

How Angels and VCs View Credit

The good news is that poor personal credit may not be a stumbling block when it comes to getting angel funding or venture capital. Jan Davis, a partner in Triangle Angel Partners (TAP), based in the Raleigh/Durham area, explains:

"Most angel investors don't check business credit reports because the businesses are so young there won't be much information available. We don't check personal credit reports either. We do, however, check references to see if the person we are dealing with is reputable. Those references might include mutual acquaintances, other angel firms, former colleagues, customers, or former and current business associates. It's similar to the way you might check someone out before you hire them for a job. But it may be a little more involved because you are giving them your money.

"If a bankruptcy or something came up but we really liked the deal, we might ask more questions. We also wouldn't be surprised if an entrepreneur was loaded up with debt because they have been funding the business for a while on their own resources. We would still expect them to manage it well and be responsible of course. We are really looking more for solid citizens."

However, Davis also warns that this viewpoint is starting to change, and that some angels are starting to consider the personal credit of the owner when conducting their due diligence. If your personal credit is poor, be prepared to have a credible explanation of what happened, and why it will not impair your ability to grow your company.

John Cambier is a managing partner with IDEA Fund Partners in Durham, North Carolina, a venture capital firm. He says that some VC's look at the owner's credit, but most don't. "We've been part of one deal where our co-investor required, and I supported, obtaining credit reports on the three founders of the company. This was one deal out of 25 over the last ten years."

At the same time, he points out that his firm has made "few investments where we haven't had or built a relationship with one or more of the company's founders over a 6 to 12 plus month period prior to investing. This has, thus far, given us a pretty reliable indicator of who we're backing, at least with respect to anything a credit report would have shed light on."

Both angels and VCs have their place in the cycle of financing new and existing business. And know that a new strategy has entered this arena…

Chapter 15

Crowdfunding

Julie made excellent bagels. They were specifically made according to an old family recipe and her customers loved them. Many travelled miles to get Julie's bagels, and when they did they asked if she would ever open more locations.

Julie had thought about expanding, but she didn't have access to a lot of money. And she had a visceral aversion to being beholden to any bank. She once asked her attorney about raising money for expansion from all her clients who wanted her to expand. That seemed like a logical way to go. But her attorney said the Securities and Exchange Commission (the "SEC"), the federal government's regulator for stock sales, didn't allow advertising to raise money.

That didn't make sense to Julie. If she could raise money from her customers she could grow her business and employ more people. Why was the government against that?

Her attorney explained that the SEC felt there were too many bad apples who took advantage of innocent investors. The SEC felt that protecting investors was more important than capital formation and business growth.

Again, this didn't make sense to Julie. She wrote to her Congressman about this. Why, she asked, when businesses want to expand, did the government prevent them from doing so? Her Congressman wrote back saying a lot of Americans were asking the same question. And he said Congress—both Democrats and Republicans—responded by passing the JOBS Act, which opened up fund raising for small business.

Julie confirmed this with her attorney. Under the new law, Julie could tell her customers about her stock offering. She could direct them to an internet portal to review her stock offering. And they could invest so she could expand so they could stop driving across town to get a bagel. Everybody won.

Crowdfunding brings together a large number of people who pool their money to support a wide range of activities. (It is sometimes also called hyperfunding or crowd financing.) In recent years, the crowd has supported disaster relief, artistic endeavors, civic activities and political campaigns. Importantly, the crowd will also fund startup companies and business projects.

There are several types of crowdfunding offered through numerous websites:

- Donations: Here, donors support a cause or person by making donations with no expectation of reward. Sites like these raise money for everything from medical bills to community projects.

- Rewards: An individual, artist or business offers specific rewards in exchange for donations. For example, a musician might raise money to produce an album and offer a copy of the album to smaller donors or a private concert for larger donors. Currently one of the most popular models, it has allowed authors, filmmakers, and inventors to raise money—in both small and large amounts—for their projects or ventures.

- Lending: This model includes P2P lenders like Lending-Club.com and Prosper.com, as mentioned in Chapter 1.

- Equity model: Money is raised from investors, who may be friends or strangers, or interested customers, as in Julie's case.

Crowdfunding is derived from crowdsourcing. Wikipedia, the free encyclopedia, is an example of crowdsourcing, where the small editorial contributions from many people are leveraged into a bigger whole, a massive compendium of information. When you add money to the concept, you have crowdfunding.

There are three key players in these models. First, you have the project initiator, who proposes the venture. Of course, you have the crowd, who will (hopefully) fund the project. And then you have the platform, which brings the two parties together.

In recent years, a number of platforms have sprung up to assist in connecting parties interested in various types of funding.

A key restriction limiting equity crowdfunding efforts for raising money for companies are the securities laws. In the years prior to the Great Depression of the 1930's, stock promoters would make whatever claim they wanted about a stock offering. They would run up a stock on wild rumors, sell their shares at the top and then let the shares fall. The scheme is called 'pump and dump.' Pump up the price and dump at the top. Once the shares fell they'd buy back in and do it all over again. As you can imagine, many unsophisticated investors were taken advantage of in these schemes.

To regulate this free-wheeling activity, the U.S. government created the Securities and Exchange Commission ("SEC") in 1933. Britain has their version in the Financial Services Authority. Most countries have an agency to deal with the bad guys who populate any stock market. The problem is that in trying to protect naïve investors, the securities laws can go overboard and prevent capital formation, which is necessary for job growth and economic advancement.

To get around these restrictive laws, entrepreneurs have sought to sell various economic interests that some felt were not defined as securities. In response, government regulators took a very broad view of what was a security.

So the question becomes, "Just what is a security?" The U.S. has a four part test:

1. An exchange of money,
2. With an expectation of profits arising from,
3. A common enterprise, and
4. Which depends solely on the efforts of a third party.

Some funding sources have dealt within these restrictions by setting up peer-to-peer lending sites, such as Funding Community, Lending Club, and Funding Circle. While loans are certainly securities under the SEC's very broad definitions, short term business loans in small amounts as offered by Funding Community are exempted. Other peer-to-peer loan sites only deal with accredited investors, as defined ahead, and thus follow the securities laws.

Other types of crowdfunding, in particular the donation and reward models, are exempt from these concerns because there is no expectation of profit from the person who is either making a donation or contributing in exchange for a specific non-financial reward. Accordingly, donating money to a new local brewery in exchange for free beer for life is not considered a security, (even though it may constitute a form of security for some alcoholic investors.)

But in the equity model of crowdfunding you most certainly do have a security. You are advancing money to a third party with the expectation of profits. As such, an issuer must either register the public offering with their government's agency (the SEC) or prepare the offering known as a Private Placement Memorandum (or "PPM") according to one of the rule-driven exemptions, such as the SEC's rule 506 of Regulation D. (For an overview of Rule 506 see Chapter 14 of Garrett's book *Start Your Own Corporation.*) A discussion of how to prepare a PPM is found in Chapter 17 ahead. Since these exempt offerings aren't public offerings they are called private placements. Failure to follow the rules for either public offerings or private placements can lead to both civil and criminal penalties.

Because crowdfunding carries so much promise for the formation of capital to help start businesses, restrictions on the securities laws were loosened by Congress in April, 2012 with the passage of the JOBS Act. But since crowdfunding also carries the risk that sharp promoters will use the new rules to separate money from less sophisticated investors the government has had to step in with regulations. The federal rules have not been finalized as of this writing yet. Note that nearly a dozen states allow for crowd funding offerings within their state (and are thus free from federal requirements). It's a changing area of the law.

For updates on new crowdfunding rules and regulations, be sure to visit the Resource Section.

While opening up crowdfunding opportunities by easing some of the rules, the JOBS Act limits the amount a crowdfunding issuer can sell to a total of $1 million of securities in any 12 month period. These securities may be sold by traditional licensed broker dealers (which is unlikely as we will see in a moment) or by the newer Funding Portals registered with the SEC.

The key element in all of this is the ability to advertise your offering to the public through a Funding Portal. While traditional broker dealers (think Smith Barney or Charles Schwab) have always been able to sell private placements directly to their clients without the need to advertise, they have never really done so. Typically, a private placement is a smaller offering involving more risk. As a smaller offering, the broker dealer can't collect a lot in fees for their due diligence review and promotion efforts. As a riskier offering, they can also run afoul with their clients when an investment goes bad.

So with a lack of private exposure through broker dealers and a prohibition against public advertising, many worthy business ventures never got funded. Without capital formation there is less job creation. The JOBS Act seeks to address the issue by allowing for the public advertising of private offerings through the Funding Portals.

Although the advertising rules are loosened, many of the more stringent Rule 506 requirements remain in effect. Of importance is the requirement to provide complete financial and other information an investor needs to make an informed decision. You will prepare a PPM that will include clear and complete information about:

- The Company
- Risk Factors
- Business and Properties
- Use of Proceeds
- Capitalization
- Offering Price Factors
- Description of Securities
- Plan of Distribution
- Dividends, Distributions and Redemptions
- Directors of the Company
- Officers and Key Personnel of the Company

- Principal Stockholders
- Management Relationships, Transactions and Remuneration
- Litigation
- Federal Tax Aspects
- Miscellaneous Factors
- Financial Statements
- Management's Discussion and Analysis of Certain Relevant Factors

The new public advertising rules for Rule 506 offerings initially only allow accredited investors to invest. An individual is accredited if they either 1) have at least $1 million in net worth excluding the primary residence or 2) have an annual income of at least $200,000 (or $300,000 if the spouse's income is counted too). A company is accredited if 1) it has at least $5 million in assets and is not formed for the purpose of making the investment or 2) if each of its owners is accredited.

Non-accredited investors are those who fall below the accredited investor standards. That is they don't have 1) a $1 million in net worth and 2) an annual income of $200,000 or more (or $300,000 a year if they are married). Remember, you can have a $1 million in net worth and not the annual income and still be an accredited investor. And vice versa. But if you don't have either then you are non-accredited. Which is fine, since the SEC is developing new rules to allow non-accredited investors to participate in crowdfunding ventures. Again, these rules haven't yet been adopted at the time of this printing.

A key crowdfunding departure from the traditional, no-advertising-allowed Rule 506 offering is the need to verify that an accredited investor is really accredited. Crowdfunders must review a potential investor's IRS forms for income verification or obtain from a registered broker-dealer or investment advisor a written confirmation of assets to ensure accredited investor status. With a traditional Rule 506, investors can simply self-certify, or state they are accredited without having to prove it.

Like any security, the issuer (the company selling the stock) and its officers and directors can be personally liable for material misstatements or omissions. This is definitely a time when you want to under-promise and over-deliver.

Fifteen days before you begin any general solicitation notice to accredited investors you must file a notice with the SEC. Again, there are myriad rules to be followed when entering into this arena.

A traditional Rule 506 offering allows an unlimited amount of money to be raised. A crowdfunding Rule 506 offering limits the amount to just $1 million in a 12 month period. So for those who want to raise larger amounts from both accredited investors, and up to 35 non-accredited but sophisticated investors, a traditional Rule 506 private placement may still be the way forward. Of course, you will work with your securities attorney no matter what route you take. The securities laws are complicated, onerous and unforgiving. You definitely want competent counsel by your side. In Chapters 16 and 17 we'll explain what you need to know about PPMs.

But as the era of crowdfunding begins, keep an eye out for opportunities to fund and grow your business with the help of your biggest fans, your loyal customers.

Three Essential Rules for Crowdfunding Campaigns

Creating and launching a successful crowdfunding campaign involves more than just setting it up and waiting for the money to roll in. Here are three key strategies for any crowdfunding campaign.

1. Know Your Target Market

When launching a crowdfunding campaign it is crucial to know your audience. Who are your customers? If you're raising money to expand an established business, then you have an advantage , as you already know some of your potential contributors. For startups with a new idea or product, being creative is critical. Research your potential audience by reading blogs and new sites. Know what the key and current issues are in your space. See what kind of content garners the most shares and comments—this is what your audience really cares about and where you should position your brand.

2. Know How Much You Need

Before raising money, you need to know exactly how much money you will need to develop your product or service, hire staff, and pay for all the related costs. Include the crowdfunding platform's commission (which can be 5 to 15 percent of the amount raised.) Expenses should be categorized as fixed or variable. Variable expenses can always go higher, so estimate high. Also understand the tax implications involved: money raised through crowdfunding is not tax-free and if you raise money one year, for example, but plan to spend some of the proceeds on production the next, you could run into a tax problem.

3. Track Activity and Adjust As Needed

All of the major crowdfunding platforms either have their own native traffic analysis tools or let you connect to a third-party solution. Once the campaign is live, review and analyze traffic data to better focus your efforts. Depending on which sources of traffic most of your supporters are coming from, whether blogs or Twitter, focus should be put into these and similar channels knowing they have higher likelihood of generating more contributions.

Crowdfunding offers a new avenue for entrepreneurs to fund their business. That said, the ongoing rules regarding securities and raising money still apply.

Which is why the next chapter is so important...

Chapter 16

Securities Law Overview

As we learned in the last chapter, there are rules for bringing in investors to fund a new or existing business. And there are strict penalties for not following those rules. So you will follow the rules, right?

We need to start by getting an explanation in place that you'll need to keep in mind. The word gets thrown around a lot, but again: Just what in the blazes are "securities"?

Once you've collected your personal savings together and borrowed where you can to get the business started, securities are the next principal tool of raising initial and ongoing basic capital funds, in equity or debt, with which the company will be able to grow in the future. Securities represent present or future rights of ownership of the company that cost the investor something, whether in time or money, and are supposed to return something to the investor, whether in distributions of profits, interest on a loan or increasing resale value over what the securities were originally worth.

Securities define ownership. Even when unissued and purely conceptual, they are very real. You can't just start printing out certificates for increasing numbers of shares as you need to raise money. (You're not the government.) Securities have a life, and laws, of their own. They stand for everything about your corporation in terms of who owns what and who controls what.

If you only issue one share of stock and issue it to your friend, your friend owns 100 percent of your company—all of it. Perhaps we should call it his company then, for you won't have another word to say about the business, unless he hires you. At the other end, though, it can be just as dangerous. Suppose you own 100 percent of the stock; every time you sell a share, your controlling percentage is accordingly diluted. And if you keep cranking out certificates for more and more shares, then increasing dilution (and resulting erosion) of value, ownership, corporate control and stability will soon follow for you and all other shareholders.

Thus, control over the company's stock, how to dole it out and the importance of keeping a lot of authorized stock (meaning unissued) in reserve are concepts to understand and analyze before issuing anything at all. For most purposes, in fact, the company is treated like a "person," with rights and liabilities, and you are in the position of caring for it—not the other way around. Moreover, from the moment you transfer a single share, you will be working for that person and every other shareholder, small or large, that will follow.

SECURITIES PREPARATION FOR A NEW BUSINESS

As you'll be seeing in this book, although securities are of vital interest to all companies, they have a special impact on newborn businesses: Something has to get you out of the starting gate for the company to survive until it can achieve strong, stable revenue streams and rely on its own income to sustain the day-to-day costs of doing business.

Unless you're loaded with old money or are terribly persuasive with bankers, the sale of securities may be the safest way to move into active operations. But beware of the circling "financiers" who may give you cash, but at a very high price, possibly even at the price of ownership and control altogether. Even later, when revenues are generating reliable income to run the business, securities may provide a secondary source of maintaining and building the company's financial foundation.

Upon incorporation, the company (remember, the company —not you) has a pile of common stock to begin with as stated in its articles of incorporation. Although this amount can be increased in the future, doing so will entail lots of obligations such as clear records that justify the increase, board and shareholder approvals, notifications to the government and interested parties, preventing shareholders from having their ownership unfairly diluted and ensuring the stability of the valuation of each share. Mainly, think of inflation. If you decide to double the number of available shares, every existing share is now only worth half of its prior value, and each investor's percentage is accordingly affected.

Good securities practice is to start with a large enough stack of stock to take care of things for a long time, and to be prudent in how you distribute it. For most businesses hoping to grow soon and steadily, 25 million to 50 million shares of authorized stock is a good amount to set forth in the articles of incorporation. This is just the conceptual pile authorized to sit in an imaginary safe until issued for one purpose or another by the board of directors. Only upon issuance does a share have actual strength, but keep that grand total in mind as you do your securities planning.

Thoughtful supervision with each share of stock in mind is an essential part of initial business organization and budgeting. Each issued share will have a changing value that, when collected together with all others, is one way of representing the total value of the company. Valuation is critical for considering the important obligations and concerns related to what rights others besides you will have in deciding how to control the condition and direction of the business.

As a whole, knowing how much of the pile of authorized stock is being delegated to each matter that arises will keep you steady in devising future control and capital-raising strategies, as well as retaining reserves for other company efforts later on, such as the development of a stock option plan for employees.

COMMON AND MORE COMMON; PREFERRED AND MORE PREFERRED

Also, in almost all cases, creating multiple kinds of stock — common and preferred — in classes and series of varying styles of benefits and burdens is generally more of a headache in initial business financial planning than a benefit. For example, some complicated offerings may have a Class A common stock voting for the entire board of directors, a Class A preferred stock that has no voting rights but a preference on monies at dissolution and then another Class B common stock that gets a vote for only one director. This might be too confusing for most start-ups. Instead, consider a single class of common stock as the easiest and most common way to begin. Later in corporate life, other classes and series of common stock are sometimes created to raise capital but alter certain rights and responsibilities of both shareholder and company.

On the other hand, one school of thought suggests that creating two initial classes of common stock is a better way to get started. The main class that will be offered and widely held is restricted to voting for a minority of members of the board of directors, perhaps even only one seat. The second class of common stock is tightly held by control-conscious founders and its holders are granted the right to vote for a majority of board positions. In this manner, control of the company would be difficult to wrest away from those who formed it.

That may sound attractive, but take a hard look at yourself and other founders first. Unless you have a strong record of reliability in successfully running a business, coupled with the ability to instill a firm trust in the first class of shareholders that the individual or small group holding majority voting control will also care for the interests of the large group with minority power, you may have a very difficult time selling shares. The Ford family has voting control over their company, but they've been selling cars for over a hundred years. We'll discuss alternative founder control issues shortly, but for now note that the tighter your grip, the less others will trust your judgment, objectivity and concern for their investment as much as your own. While issuance of securities involves control issues, you don't want to go so far as to make ownership in your company unattractive to investors.

Preferred stock is the more frequent second vehicle created after using a single class of common stock, and the preferences may command a higher price per share, though usually this is more true for a public company or a private company that is showing strong profits. "Preferred" refers to certain kinds of preferential treatment for these shareholders. The two most frequent preferences are:

- The right to receive dividends from profits made on investments before common stock shareholders, who must wait to see if any distributions remain for them after payment to the preferred stockholders is allocated

(Then again, in a business' early stages, how likely is the ability to offer dividends of any kind really going to be?); and

- Preferential treatment if the company dissolves, such that remaining funds, if any, after all dissolution and winding up matters are completed may be allocated first to the preferred shareholders (again, with common stockholders waiting to see if anything is left for them at the end of the list).

Still, most voting rights remain with the main class of common stock. Removing this right frequently has an adverse impact on the attractiveness of the stock for subsequent transfers, and corporate shareholder voting matters could become too tightly controlled by a small group of preferred holders (a bad prospect for both the common shareholders and company management).

However, all this is still off in your future.

For now, just get a grip on the importance of each share and the life it has of its own, with you in custody. Keeping the rights that accompany shares in mind will guide you through your corporate career—that and understanding the philosophy of why and how securities are regulated, both while in your hands and whenever you distribute them.

Let's get back to the beginning with you and the gang: the founders. Your first obligation is to keep the company safe from those who might want to grab control of it away from the people whose mission gave it its first breath. Thus, the founders need to have enough of an ownership interest to make sure they have the power to protect the company. This control is ensured by issuing founders' shares. The standard price per share is the stated par value of the common stock (in fact, today that's about the only real meaning left for assigning a par value to the shares at all). Remember that the typical par value is $0.001 per share, or one-tenth of one cent per share. So if you're going to issue yourself 1 million founders' shares, you'll need to contribute something of value equal to $1,000 into the company's coffers. (One million shares times $0.001 per share equals $1,000, right?) For example, in Nevada, the contribution can be in the form of cash, property, a promissory note, or services you've rendered or are rendering in the start-up stage. Not all states are that flexible, so be sure to check your local rules. However, if allowed, it's easy to see how $1,000 in services could be rendered by getting the company up and running.

Keep in mind that you can't issue shares for less than par value. Moreover, it's good practice to state a par value in your Articles of Incorporation rather than stating "no par value." Let's use Nevada again as an example. You have fees associated with your authorized number of shares. If you give your shares no par value, the Nevada Secretary of State's office will give them a deemed value of $1 per share for fee calculation purposes and charge a hefty fee for it all. Your money is better spent elsewhere, so use par value.

There are two very important points, besides safe control, that you need to know about founders' shares. These two things will never apply to your stock again. First, the par value price tag. Never again will you be issuing shares for $0.001 each. From here on out, you need to raise real money to get the Company going. Bring in the founders at a low par value price and then charge everyone else more.

Second, the founder's round is the one and only time you can issue shares without the legal obligation to create a formal offering memorandum and obtain signed subscription agreements. After this moment, securities law demands that you begin treating securities with the underlying principles of protecting the widows and orphans and giving every investor adequate full disclosure about your company and its securities. Let's take a closer look at these two points about founders' shares.

JUSTIFYING THE LOW PRICE OF FOUNDERS' SHARES

There are two main facts that justify such a small price tag for founders, and they are unlikely to occur again: First, these are the people who, from the beginning, have already invested a lot on a big risk, usually including both financial aid and much time and effort expended in "sweat equity" for the company. Second, at this point of the company's new birth, it's hard to support the conclusion that the business is actually worth much of anything yet in its own right.

The founders are investing and risking a lot of themselves and their money in what is still but a dream. Of all who may come along in the future, they are the most likely to remain faithful to the origin and objectives laid out at the company's inception. In consideration for what they are risking with little assurance, they have the greatest justification for receiving a high return as the company and the value of its shares grow with time. This is where Mom came into the picture. She can invest as a founder and in turn have the chance of high rewards as the company grows and its securities increase in value.

However, don't call Mom just yet, for this brings us to a discussion of the second attribute applicable to founders' shares alone. This is the one and only time you can distribute shares without having to give each person a well-crafted offering memorandum and without getting their signature on a subscription agreement. Why? Think back to the SEC's concern about adequate full disclosure.

YOUR ONE AND ONLY OPPORTUNITY TO AVOID A WRITTEN OFFERING

Presumably, the founders who are putting the thing together already know just about everything there is to know about the company. They know what it will do, what the competition is like, what your business' plan of attack in the field will be, how much (or little) money the company has, how much more financial assistance you'll be needing each step of the way, and all the risks involved. At this point, these founders know it's a risk of everything. All their hard work and financial input could vanish overnight.

So why would the government be concerned about written disclosures? The founders should know the risks of the struggling new company and the business plan that they hope will make it all work out. Remember, the SEC has no grave concern about whether someone makes a good investment— just that they should have all the information with which to do so knowingly.

Mom may be the one and only person on earth who would hand over her money to you in complete faith. But even if Mom is such a prize, that's not enough for the SEC. Does Mom —or any other pure-cash investing founder—really know the business that well? Is she armed with the same understanding of the likelihood of losing everything?

If you can't be sure—if the SEC wouldn't be sure—have Mom and other family and friends wait for your first round offering for traditional investors. It's only a nickel a share, re-member? But it comes with full disclosure—something you owe every investor. Think about it. If anyone's worth protecting by ensuring they know the whole story, it's those you feel closest to. And doing so will keep them close.

There are lots of ways to slice a pie. Personalities and per-formance potential are good guideposts, but ultimately every founder is giving in. Everyone will want a lot, including you, but no one will win alone. Don't spread the stock too thinly across too many people. The objective, aside from rewards, is to keep your boat afloat.

The founders must be comprised of a few people who work well together, believe in each other as much as they believe in the dream and will have the tenacity tempered by prudent judgment that will help keep the life-raft steady and spirits up while you set out upon a sometimes treacherous sea. Take your time in putting these people together. You'll need to be sure they're all the kind of people who can sit through the stills and remain sturdy through the storms during a long period with little space and little food to go around. Who do you want to be in a life-raft with?

RESIST THE URGE TO OVER-CONTROL

A final point about founders: Resist the urge to over-control the company by issuing too much stock to yourselves. You not only need to trust each other; you're going to need to trust many other owners, as well. And that's a problem with a company founded and funded with securities. Everyone needs to work and play well with others, for every share means actual owner-ship of the business. If other owners are so heavily outweighed by a tight few, arguments over respect for the minority are sure to follow. Don't go down that path.

Too tight a hand also strangles your securities. Think about the ongoing nature of your successive offerings to an increasing pool of people. As your company grows, you won't have 51 percent anymore unless you keep issuing the founders more shares in some manner. Are you going to keep doing that on into eternity? It ties up increasingly large sums of your authorized stock for which little if any capital is raised.

Second, it's a tough sell to investors, for the further away they come from the old trusted friends and family, the harder it will be for them to accept the idea that they have no real say in the company's operations—and the bigger their investment, the more this bugs them. I've dealt with investors who will not touch a company in which one or two (or more) founders own 60 percent of the company. They simply (and perhaps, prudently) don't want to put money into a business (especially a new one without proven skills of the founders) where the company is too tightly or unrealistically controlled. Thus, just as it is dangerous to let too much control slip out of your hands too early, similarly, with too much control you can drive away much-needed capital.

Over-control can also give an unexpected impression to the outside world. What you see as stability in a trusted group may wind up being perceived as greed and a suspicious nature. Stand in a potential outside investor's shoes for the moment. Would you want to hand over your savings to people like that?

There's another common but incorrect impression you could set up unexpectedly. Sometimes potential investors will wonder if such control-fanaticism isn't really a sign of inexperienced founders who fear they'll get tossed the more they're watched and the more they must answer to others. Remember the justification that you'll be putting in your business plan for why you are qualified to run the show. Qualifications will increasingly become a far more serious topic of scrutiny, especially if tight control suggests self-doubt. Large trustworthy investments could evaporate into thin air.

BUT DON'T GIVE AWAY ALL CONTROL EITHER

On the other hand, there's good reason to justify hanging on to the 51 percent block through the early life of your business. Not all investors will prove to be great friends and allies. People who put in a lot often want a lot of respect and deference with regard to their demands as prominent shareholders—especially if they pass into a sizable minority shareholder range, say 10 percent. They can believe they're entitled to a private phone line right to your desk and 24 hour rights to your home phone number, to boot.

They can even form alliances with others and attempt to wrest away control of the company on the suspicion that you just don't see the importance of getting the most for the shareholders first. They'll argue that you're just too tight-fisted, pouring profits back into the business when distributions are to their better liking or perhaps that you're too timid to take the company public as soon as possible to give them a certain "exit strategy."

At the right time, both distribution of some profits and the thrill of going public can definitely be in order, but not every one of your company's owners will necessarily see the big picture. Especially during the vulnerable first years of the company's life, majority control among founders is a good guard, provided you and the gang stick together. Keep an eye out, for some large investors like to wedge themselves into potential fractures in the group, carry a few over to their side, and wham: the 51 percent is a thing of the past.

There's no need to feel overwhelmed by this. Your best defense is a straight-forward three-part approach: care in assembling the founding members, care in keeping investors informed of the company's progress and care in creating and regularly revising your business plan so that results speak for themselves. There's no better protection for your fledgling company than giving it your best and doing a good job.

Let's delve deeper into your PPM...

Chapter 17

Private Placement Offerings

Regulation D, Rule 506 Private Placement Offerings

Financing your business or real estate venture may involve raising money from others—friends, family and the like. It can be a good way to go, but you've got to be careful. You've got to use the right procedures and documents. A properly prepared private placement memorandum (PPM) is the correct way to legally raise money from investors.

In Chapter 14 of Garrett's book *Start Your Own Corporation* we presented an overview for raising money for your business. Frequently, this involves preparation of a PPM. In this chapter we'll discuss the nuts and bolts of putting together a PPM.

While there are several fund raising rules to consider using, we will focus on a Regulation D, Rule 506, or "Rule 506 offering". This allows your company to either raise an unlimited amount of money during the term of your offering or, when using a crowdfunding Rule 506, to advertise and raise $1 million during a 12 month period. In either one your PPM is not, as a rule, subject to review at either the state or the federal level.

Because of their simplicity, and the lack of review, Rule 506 offerings are easily the most popular way for new and existing businesses to raise money. And with the advent of crowdfunding, almost everyone will be using Rule 506. So the information in this chapter is important to know.

But before we get to drafting the document, we need to clear up a few preliminary questions:

1. Is Your Company's Minute Book Up to Date?

Your Minute Book is a written history of your corporate existence. The Minute Book contains a company's Articles of Incorporation, bylaws (or Articles of Organization and Operating Agreement if you operate as an LLC), annual reports filed with various state or provincial government agencies, registers of directors, officers and stockholders, business and biographical question-naires for its directors and officers, minutes of directors and stockholders meetings, and, in some cases, copies of major contracts entered into by the company.

The Minute Book tells the story of your company and is much more important than you may think, particularly when you are attempting to raise capital. If you present an investor who is considering investing any amount of money into your company with a Minute Book containing a copy of your Articles of Incorporation, a draft copy of your bylaws (which you meant to get signed, but never quite got around to), two or three file-stamped annual reports and pro-forma annual meeting minutes for your directors and officers, that investor may think twice before parting with their money.

It is a guarantee that at some point an investor considering investing a significant sum into your company is going to have their own attorney and is going to want that attorney to conduct due diligence on your company. (Due diligence being an in-vestigation into your company and its business, to prove to an investor that you are who you say you are and your company is worth what you say it is worth.) Part of the due diligence process is reviewing your company's Minute Book to see if you are able to keep your house in order.

Just in terms of basic corporate formalities it is key for all companies to have a full and complete Minute Book. We are continually amazed at how many companies fail to keep these documents properly updated—if they have them at all. You need to keep the Minute Book updated to avoid piercing the corporate veil. Piercing the veil is where a creditor shows you didn't follow the corporate formalities (like keeping up your Minute Book) and thus you should be held personally responsible for the corporation's debts. Piercing the veil is successful in almost half of all cases, meaning that many companies are lax on corporate formalities. Please keep your Minute Book up to date. Your Minute Book must be current if you are going to raise money from investors. (If your Minute Book needs work see the Resource Section for corporate clean up assistance.)

2. Where are your Material Contracts?

A material contract is a significant contract that your company has entered into and which directly affects its ability to operate. Examples of material contracts include the lease(s) or mortgage(s) for your company's office, warehouse or manufacturing premises, agreements for your company to buy or sell property or other assets, trademark registrations, patent applications, vehicle leases, sales agreements, employment-related agreements (such as consulting, employment, confidentiality, management and/or stock options), expert reports, legal opinions and the written consents of auditors, experts and counsel for your company to use or incorporate materials prepared by said individuals into other documentation (such as PPMs).

What is and isn't a material contract can be quite subjective. While your payment agreement with Office Depot for the company's office supply account is not going to be considered a material contract another more comprehensive vendor agreement may rise to material importance.

Keep all of your material contracts in a safe place and be ready to review them with a potential investor.

3. Who Will Your Company Offer Securities To?

Accredited investors are individuals or companies worth $1 million or more in assets (excluding home and furnishings, for individuals) and annual income of $200,000 or more (or $300,000 combined with a spouse) for each of the past three years. Non-accredited investors are individuals or businesses that don't meet the accredited investor income and asset tests. Purchaser representative-assisted investors are non-accredited investors who purchase securities based on the advice of their financial advisor, and Regulation S investors are individuals or companies who are not U.S. residents (or, in other words, foreign investors). So before you start drafting the PPM let's understand who it is directed towards. As they say in show business, and which applies to all activities: "Know your Audience."

4. Is Your Company Planning to Sell Securities to Non-Accredited Investors or Through Crowdfunding? Have You Arranged for the Preparation of Audited Financial Statements?

Whenever non-accredited investors are involved, audited financial statements, audited to a date within 135 days of the date of your PPM, will be required—except in special circumstances. Where your company is a successor entity to another business, financial statements for that previous entity are also required and can be consolidated into your existing company's operations. The financial statements must be prepared to US GAAP standards (Generally Accepted Accounting Principles). They should cover the previous two fiscal years, or less, where your company is a new entity without a financial history. Unaudited interim quarterly statements will also be required (prepared to your company's most recent fiscal quarter-end). Financial statements must be prepared in comparative form, contrasting current information against that from previous years. I know this sounds daunting. Be sure to work with your CPA on these issues.

Special Circumstances for Waiver of Audited Financial Statement Requirements.

It is sometimes possible to proceed with selling securities under a PPM to non-accredited investors without financial statements. If your company cannot obtain full audited financial statements without unreasonable effort or expense, then you may provide financial statements where only the balance sheet has been audited, as long as the balance sheet is audited to a date within 120 days of the date of your PPM.

What constitutes "unreasonable effort or expense," is not clearly defined, most likely because this is an area that is best reviewed on a case-by-case basis. You can safely rule out "because we don't want to," or any derivative of that reason, though. The best standard to apply is "Would an experienced and prudent executive corporate officer consider the expense to be unreasonable?" Some examples may be that:

- Your company's records had been lost in a fire or other accident and the cash wasn't immediately available to have them replaced; or

- Your company is in a critical financial position, and cannot afford to have a full audit completed, but will not be able to continue operations without the ability to raise some equity capital.

If your company is in doubt, please be sure to check with your securities attorney and explain the issues facing your company and why it is unable to have audited financial statements prepared.

Audit Rules for Crowdfunding

The best way to illustrate the audit rules for crowdfunding is found in this next chart:

Financial Conditions and Requirements for Issuers	
Issuer's Financial Condition	**Related Requirements**
$100,000 or less	a) Most recent annual income tax returns filed by issuer b) Financial statements, certified by principal executive officer
Greater than $100,000 but not greater than $500,000	a) Financial statements reviewed by an independent public accountant
Greater than $500,000	a) Audited financial statements

Again, be sure to work with your CPA before proceeding.

With these preliminary issues resolved, let's look towards preparing the PPM.

Assembling the PPM material

The next stage is to assemble the information that will be included in your company's PPM. Please know that we have included a sample PPM in the Appendix. This template should only be used in concert with the services of an experienced securities attorney. But after reading this chapter and reviewing the template you'll have a much better idea of what a PPM is and how it can help you finance your business.

1. How Much Money do You Need?

After working through the preliminary questions, the next and most important thing to consider when planning your company's Rule 506 offering is how much money your company needs. Ideally, at this stage you have completed your company's business plan and know how much it is going to cost to complete the development of your product (or service) and bring it to market, and you will have a detailed business development timeframe.

In some cases this sum of money is going to be fairly substantial (let's say $2 million). That's a significant amount to try and raise up-front, particularly if up to this point your company has been largely you, your brilliant idea and a lot of sweat equity. As is often the case, though, at this stage you may not have anything concrete to show to a potential investor.

However, while the full $2 million is a somewhat intimidating number, it may be that you can get your company's business going without the full $2 million in the bank right now.

2. How Much Money do You Need Right Now?

Take another look at your company's business plan and financial projections, assuming that no angel investor is going to drop in and drop off the $2 million you need. Try breaking your company's business plan down into stages and determine how much money is needed for each stage. What does your company need to accomplish over the next six months, and how much money will it cost? After that first six-month period, what will your company's capital needs be for the following six or twelve month period, and where will your company's business development be during those same time periods?

There is a very good possibility that by breaking down your company's business development into six or twelve month stages, you can break down the overall capital funding requirement into smaller, much less intimidating chunks. And remember, with crowdfunding, you can only raise $1 million in any one 12 month period anyway.

As an example, let's assume you are developing a software application that you foresee becoming a part of everyone's daily computing life. The production timeline for the software has been designed, the source code has been written, and you have a rough, preliminary program assembled that you can demonstrate to computer-savvy professionals to illustrate the overall concept of your company's software. It's not quite ready to go to the beta-testing market, but your home is mortgaged to the hilt and you don't have any more money to give at this point. You need help from outside investors if you are going to push forward.

After working through your company's business plan, you have projected that you can finish the software, complete the beta testing and debugging stages, and have the finalized version ready for distribution in eighteen months, coinciding with the Christmas season. You have also projected that in order to meet that eighteen-month time frame, your company is going to need $1.5 million dollars. Unfortunately, neither you nor your family has those kinds of financial resources. However, you do have friends and colleagues in the software industry and being that you all speak the same language, you believe that you can sell them on the potential of your company's software.

So, by carefully analyzing your company's business plan, you begin to break it down into development stages. You know already that the software is going to need another three months to work out the early bugs. You believe that it will then be ready to be distributed to a wider audience for the purpose of beta-testing it and reporting back on all problems they may encounter, and you believe this will take another two months. To complete the testing and debugging of the software to the point where it is stable enough to go to market will be another two months, for a total of seven months. This stage, Stage 1, you have calculated will cost you $350,000 in programming and development costs, and to have the program readied and distributed to beta-testers. If all goes well, at the conclusion of Stage 1 you should be in a position to begin the heavy mass-market advertising and promotional campaign that will be required to make your company and its software a household name.

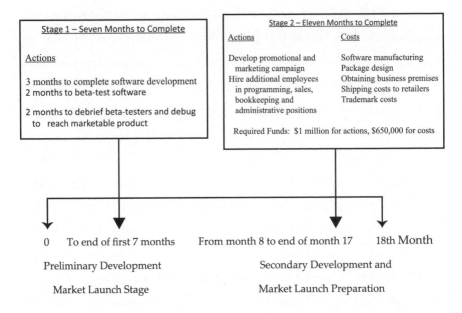

That stage, Stage 2, you have calculated will take up the bulk of the total funds your company needs, or $1 million even. The remaining $650,000 will also be required in Stage 2 for manufacturing costs, packaging design, drop-shipments to retailers across North America, securing suitable business premises (you can't work in your basement forever), hiring a couple of young, hungry, programmers to assist with new product developments, three to four salespeople who can cover North America, a bookkeeper to run your books and an administrative assistant to keep everything in order.

You decide that the best way to approach your company's financing requirements is to structure a Rule 506 private placement offering into two stages. The first offering, the "Stage 1 Offering" will be for the initial $350,000 needed. A portion of the Stage 1 Offering proceeds will be set aside to prepare your Stage 2 Offering, for the larger portion of funds needed, being $1.65 million. You believe that your colleagues and their friends in the software industry will see the value of your company's program and raising the initial $350,000 among them won't be that difficult. In fact, you are considering trying to kill two birds with one stone, and asking your company's Stage 1 investors to also double as your beta-testers. You figure that by shipping a CD along with their stock certificates, you can save some money on postage and mailing costs. And, by having a debugged and finished product as well as valuable feedback and market research from your industry peers, who have also acted as your beta-testers, you can present your company's Stage 2 investors with a cleaner, more polished product. This in turn will allow you to focus on selling your company's product, and showing potential Stage 2 investors where the money will come from—and when.

3. Use of Proceeds

Having determined that your company's Stage 1 Offering must raise $350,000, you now need to break this amount down a little further, and create a "Use of Proceeds" for the PPM. The Use of Proceeds section is where you break down, for the benefit of your company's investors, where the money you hope to raise is going to go. You do not have to go into extensive detail in this section, but you should break it down into at least four categories.

An example of the Use of Proceeds breakdown for your company's PPM could look something like this:

| (a) | Completion of first product development phase, including trademark/patent fees | $165,000 |
| (b) | Initial production run costs, including materials, packaging and postage/mailing costs | $85,000 |

(c)	Commissions	$35,000
(d)	Costs of the offering (including legal, accounting and audit costs, printing and state filing fees)	$30,000
(e)	Reserve for working capital (including costs for second round of financing)	35,000
	Total	$350,000

Completion of first product development phase including trademark fees — These costs relate to the hard costs of completing the beta-test version of your company's software program. They include fees paid to other consulting programmers. They also include the fees payable to your attorneys to trademark your company's product logo and patent your intellectual property.

Initial Production Run Costs, including materials, packaging and postage costs — These costs relate to what it will cost your company to design a logo, design packaging, and arrange for the production of the initial beta-test product run of its software. The postage costs, you hope, could be minimized by using your company's investors as beta-testers, and providing evaluation copies of your company's software along with stock certificates.

Commission — You may or may not pay commissions on your company's Stage 1 Offering. If you are using a venture capital firm, or an investment finder firm to help you in finding investors, you can pretty much guarantee paying a cash commission of around 10 percent, and likely giving up a portion of equity in your company. In many instances, investment finder firms take a 10/10 approach, meaning the finders will receive a cash fee equal to 10 percent of the total dollar value of sales made through them, together with a stock grant equal to 10 percent of the number of securities sold through them. However, this only applies to investments the finders secure for you. If you sell the Stage 1 Offering on your own, then no commission will be payable on the portion that you sell, and that commission money you have set aside can be folded back into your company and allocated to one or more other areas.

Please know that not just anyone can act as a finder nor can your company pay commissions or finder's fees to just anyone. It is a constant source of problems for the SEC and state securities regulators, and the rules surrounding this are both complex and strict. The rules are also fluid and can change depending on the type of private placement offering your company is conducting—so be careful and plan accordingly. This is another area that features severe penalties for misdoings. Unless you are working with a licensed broker dealer, do not offer a commission. Be sure to work with your securities attorney on this issue.

Costs of the offering (including legal, accounting and audit costs, printing and state filing fees)—There is absolutely no getting around the fact that it is going to cost you and your company to conduct the Stage 1 Offering. You need an attorney to help you craft the PPM, to make sure that you have provided full, accurate and plain disclosure to all potential investors, and to manage the follow-up regulatory filings with federal and state agencies required as investments come in. Your company can expect to spend $12,000 or more on attorney's fees for this stage, but know that it will be money well spent. This PPM may form the basis of future PPM documents—and if your company is laying its foundation for business success, it may as well be a secure and solid foundation. You may also need to pay for an audit at this stage. Work with your attorney on this requirement.

Printing fees make up the balance of this amount. A properly drafted PPM that also contains financial statements, financial projections and subscription documents can be anywhere from 30 to 60 pages or more in length. Assuming you intend to distribute 50 to 60 copies or more, you will incur copying costs. And if you want to get fancy with covers, binding and colors, the costs could be higher.

Reserve for working capital (including costs for second round of financing)—Working capital is your emergency fund. In the early stages of a company's development, anything and every thing can and will happen. If your company's capital is stretched too thinly, you may "lose your kingdom for the want of a horse-shoe nail." A contingency reserve fund is a very good thing to have. Again, it also presents your company's investors with a picture that you are thinking ahead, and carefully planning for unforeseen difficulties. In this amount you can also include the portion of funds your company will spend for its Stage 2 Offering (more legal fees and printing costs). However, with any luck your company's Stage 2 PPM will cost less than your Stage 1 PPM, as you will be in the position of updating a fairly recent document, rather than reinventing the wheel.

One thing to note here is that while it is perfectly acceptable to use a portion of the proceeds from your company's offering to pay down its accrued debts, where that portion is 10 percent or more of the gross proceeds you are required to disclose that fact to potential investors. You will also need to provide additional information, such as the full amount of the debt, to whom it is owed, the interest rate, if any, when the debt is (or was) due to be repaid, and what your company did with the money it received.

The reverse is also required. If your company is going to use more than 10 percent of its offering to acquire assets, you will also need to disclose this in your company's PPM, along with details about from whom your company is purchasing the assets and whether that individual or entity is connected to your company. As well, exactly what your company is purchasing and how the cost of the purchase is being calculated must be disclosed. For example, if one of the things your company is purchasing is the software that you developed you'd better let everyone know.

4. The Securities Being Offered

Common stock, preferred stock, convertible debentures or warrants? It's up to you. However, given that in our example the Stage 1 offering is for only $350,000, and the significant funding amount is anticipated to come from the Stage 2 offering, you may want to consider a simple common stock offering of, say, 700,000 shares of common stock at 50 cents per share. You can (and it is recommended that you do) put a minimum investment amount requirement on your company's PPM. This amount doesn't have to be too high—you don't want to scare off any non-accredited investors, but at the same time, you only have room for 35 non-accredited investors under Rule 506, and if they all come in at $2,000 each, that $70,000 won't really help your company. If you put in a required minimum investment amount of $10,000, that would ensure that even if every single one of your company's potential investors were unaccredited, you would still raise the $350,000 needed. And, if you add a disclaimer allowing for the right to accept less than a full minimum investment amount, you give your company additional flexibility without seriously compromising your ability to raise money.

Once you have selected the type of security your company is going to offer, you must make sure to describe that security in detail. If your company is offering common stock you will need to describe that stock, including what the voting rights are, whether dividends will be paid on the common stock and whether stockholders will receive any special pre-emption rights. (A pre-emption right is a right for a stockholder to be allowed to participate in all future securities offerings, so that they may ensure that his or her present ownership percentage remains the same.)

If your company elects to offer preferred stock, describe the stock features. Discuss the special rights and restrictions that may be in place, the preferential liquidation rights (if any) over common stock, any special redemption rights (where preferred stock is sold back to a company), whether the preferred stock will have voting rights or will be entitled to receive dividends. If there is a conversion feature, how the conversion feature may be activated and whether the right to convert preferred stock rests with your company, the investor or a combination of the two.

If your company is offering warrants, you will need to explain what the underlying securities consist of, how long the warrants will be exercisable (two years is the maximum), the exercise costs, if there are any forced exercise provisions (i.e., in the event your company decides to go public) and the procedure for exercising the warrants.

If your company is offering convertible debentures or other debt securities, you will need to set out when the convertible debentures mature, the interest rate and any conversion or redemption features. You will also need to set out any sub-

ordinate provisions, limitations on dividend declarations, restrictions on the ability of your company to conduct further
debt-securities offerings and whether or not your company is
required to maintain a certain asset to debt ratio.

5. Share Information

Offering Price—Because your company is a private company,
you will need to tell potential investors how you arrived at the
fifty cents per share offering price and what factors went into
that decision. With no established market for your company's
securities, there is limited or no opportunity for an investor to
conduct an independent valuation, and so your explanation
will become very important.

Dilution—You may also need to discuss the dilution factor,
which is a decrease in value of a security and/or a decrease
in an investor's overall percentage of ownership. In a typical
private company situation, a significant amount of stock will
have been issued to the founders, either for cash, services or
for assets put into the company, usually at the very low price
of one tenth of one cent. The founders will have been issued a
large amount of stock, so that they can maintain control as the
company grows and sells more securities. Dilution will occur
when additional stock is sold.

For example, if your company is worth, on paper, $100,000
and you have 10 million shares of common stock issued, then
each share is worth one cent. You and the company's directors
and officers hold 5.15 million shares of common stock. The
remaining 4.85 million common shares are owned by several
early-stage investors. Now, if you sell 2 million additional
shares of common stock at ten cents per share, for proceeds of
$200,000, but use that money for product development expenses,

it will not show up in your company's financial statements as increasing the overall value of your company. Therefore, the value of the 2 million shares will be recalculated downwards, meaning that the stockholders who participated in the offering will have already lost money just by investing in your company. Dilution is to be expected in the beginning of a company's existence and most investors will take it in stride. But if your company continues to finance itself solely through private placement offerings, without having any offsetting revenues, the investors are sure to ask questions.

Here's another example of why monitoring the dilution factor is important. You and your company's directors and officers held 5.15 million shares of common stock before the offering, which is 51.5 percent of your company's outstanding stock, which effectively gives you control of your company. However, after completing the 2 million share private placement, that 5.15 million share block has now been reduced from 51.5 percent to 42.9 percent. You have just lost your voting control of the company.

Recent Sales of Unregistered Securities—You must set out a complete record of how many shares in your company have been issued to date over the past three years and at what value. This does not have to be broken down on an investor-by-investor basis, but rather you can use a chronology of stock issuances.

Plan of Distribution—If your company's Rule 506 offering is being sold through a registered broker-dealer or if you are being assisted in selling the offering through an investment finder firm or a venture capital firm, you must set out complete details of the arrangements with such individuals. Include how much commission they will be paid and how much (if any) equity they will receive in your company. If these individuals are related to your company in any way, that relationship must be disclosed in full. Where your company's offering is being sold by you and your directors, officers and key management personnel, no commission or equity is payable, and you must make a statement to that effect.

Market for Common Equity and Related Stockholder Matters— For private companies, there is no market for securities resales. However, where your company is a public company listed on the a stock exchange, then you must tell investors where your company's securities are traded, and provide the high and low prices for your company's securities for the past eight fiscal quarters.

6. Directors, Officers, Management and Related-Transaction Information

Five-year Biographical History—Part of the PPM disclosure requirements include a five-year history for each of your company's directors, officers and key management personnel (those who can make decisions affecting the course of business for the company). The five-year disclosure must include the names, ages, addresses and positions within the company for each of these people, and a chronological listing of all of their previous employers and positions. This disclosure can be set out in either table form, narrative form or a combination of both. You must also set out whether any of your company's directors, officers and key management personnel are related to each other, and if they are, what the nature of that relationship is. And, finally, you must set out whether yourself or any of your company's key personnel have been or are subject to legal proceedings including bankruptcy, criminal charges and securities violations.

Knowing of this disclosure requirement, consider carefully who will be acting as your company's key personnel. Cousin

Benny may be an excellent businessman, but will his DUI conviction cause the investors to see your company as a greater investment risk? It will depend on your company's individual circumstances, but as a general rule it is not the best idea to have individuals with these outstanding issues on your board.

One alternative is to have a business advisory board, made up of individuals who assist your company in various ways, from offering advice to providing their services (ideally on a part-time, per-project basis). If you are faced with the problem of needing someone to assist you in developing your company's business, but that individual comes with some baggage, then consider involving them with your company in the business advisory role. That way, this individual can be involved and may be paid and receive other benefits, such as participating in incentive stock option plans, but the disclosure aspects will be minimized.

Finally, remember also that this disclosure requirement only goes back for the five preceding years. You can always move someone up to the board of directors after this five-year period has passed, but remember—their past may still come back to haunt the company.

Insider Ownership—You must set out a chart detailing the complete securities ownership position of each of your key personnel and insiders (stockholders holding 5 percent or more of your company's outstanding stock). Include common and preferred stock, outstanding warrants, incentive stock options and convertible debentures. This chart must include the ownership percentage for each individual calculated before and again after the offering. Where your company has "controlling stockholders" (a stockholder with a 10 percent or greater interest in your company's securities), and the offering will have any impact on those stockholders' positions, or if a new control position will be created as a result of the Rule 506 offering, then you must set out these details as well.

Executive Compensation—You must identify how much certain individuals are making, including stock grants, options, and the like. The disclosure relates to the "Named Executive Officers," which can be defined to mean your company's chief executive officer, likely your company's president, and the senior vice-presidents (if your company has any).

On the face of it, this may seem somewhat intrusive but if you look at it also from an investor's point of view you can see why the requirement is there. If your company is looking to raise $1.5 million, but is planning on spending $1 million of that on director and officer salaries, then how committed is your company to pushing forward with its business development? Who would want to invest so you and your buddies can buy fast cars?

This does not mean that you aren't allowed to compensate yourself and your key people fairly—there is nothing inherently improper in allowing for appropriate market-level compensation. The key, however, is to determine when that compensation will kick in. It may be the wiser choice for start-up companies and young, developing companies to have management agreements in place with all of their key personnel whereby all or a large portion of salaries are deferred until the company has become profitable, or to grant these individuals an option to take accrued salaries in stock on a yearly basis. Investors want to see commitment and sacrifice.

Management Agreements —Even though your company is your brainchild and you have absolutely no intention of walking away, not everyone has such faith. So it is still important to make sure that you and your other directors, officers and key management personnel have entered into proper management

211

agreements with your company. This way, you can set out details, such as how and when you will be compensated for your hard work, what each management team member's responsibilities within your company will be and how a management team member may leave (or be terminated by) your company. There is a discussion on employment issues, including how they relate to your company's founders and key management personnel, in Chapter 5 of *Run Your Own Corporation*.

By having management agreements in place your company is demonstrating to potential investors that it is following the proper steps and your company's management team is maintaining a level of professionalism. It demonstrates that you and your management team have made a commitment to your company. And, as in our example, unless someone else could step into your shoes and complete the software development without you, you need to assure potential investors that you aren't going to disappear at a critical point in your company's business development. A well-drafted management contract can accomplish this.

If your management contract is crafted properly (particularly where you are also the founder of your company and have the most to lose), then it could ensure that you either stay in control of your company as it grows, or are handsomely-compensated for stepping (or being pushed) aside. Remember, by offering securities in your company, you are offering slices of ownership control to the outside world. It may very well be that someone will come along who wants the whole pie and is just crafty enough to get it. With a healthy compensation arrangement in place, should the unthinkable happen and you wind up being forced out of your company in a stockholder vote, you can float gently down to the beach on your golden parachute and sip mai-tais while you plot your revenge.

Related-Transactions/Relationships—Related transactions and relationships deal with situations where your company is involved with its directors, officers, insiders or other key personnel outside the scope of their original relationships. For example, if your company's president also owns the office building where your company's offices are located, and your company is (or will be) paying rent to this person, then it is a related-party transaction. It must be disclosed in your company's PPM, particularly when the rent does not form a part of the president's remuneration for their duties and is additional monies received. Similarly, if you and two or three other directors and officers own a separate business entity specializing in software marketing over the Internet, and you want to use this business entity to market your company's software, then this relationship must be disclosed to your investors. Include the details of such an agreement, including the term of the arrangement and the consideration this business entity will receive. You will also need to provide the details on how you arrived at the amount of compensation to be paid in this related-party transaction.

Part of the philosophy behind this is a continuation of the requirement for all directors, officers and key management personnel to fully disclose how they will be compensated for their efforts on behalf of your company. And again, this is not to say that you can't enter into these types of arrangements —you just need to make sure that your company's potential investors are made aware that the relationship exists.

Another part of this philosophy is to make sure that your company's key personnel don't accidentally (or purposefully) transgress corporate opportunity requirements. A "corporate opportunity" is a business opportunity that could potentially be undertaken by your company. It is a well-established legal principle that your directors, officers and key management personnel who are offered such opportunities must bring these opportunities to the company first, before deciding to undertaken them through separate means. In other words, say a colleague of yours has been writing a software application that could dovetail nicely with the one you have developed. He has decided not to continue with it, but has offered the half-written program to you for a very attractive price. You cannot legally accept this offer, purchase his half-written software and start up a separate business venture to develop it. You are, rather, bound by the doctrine of corporate opportunity to bring the offer to your company and have the matter voted upon by your company's board of directors. (Because you are personally involved, you aren't allowed to vote). If your company's board of directors turns the purchase opportunity down, however, then you may be free to undertake the purchase on your own.

7. Company Information

Believe it or not, most of the information we have previously set out is secondary to the information contained in this section. With your input, the previous information can be prepared by your attorney. This next section, however, is and should be considered the primary responsibility of you and your company.

This section contains the history of your company, the details of the product or service it is offering, what is needed to complete product or service development, and the sales and marketing strategy. It also includes how your company will proceed to move forward if it receives the funding it needs, when your company's product or service is to hit the market, who your company will be competing against and how your company is going to succeed.

As we stated at the beginning, much of this information should be contained in your company's business plan, and if your company doesn't have a business plan or can't answer all of the questions in this section, then it may not be the right time to be seeking outside investors just yet. (Consider reading Garrett's book *Writing Winning Business Plans* first.)

Remember, once your company has outside investors, you become accountable to them. If you don't have a clear business strategy and can't "show them the money," things are going to get uncomfortable for you quickly.

There is a lot of information contained in this section. Following the next two items, we have left most of it in bullet point, as it is fairly self-explanatory.

Description of Business and Company History—Provide the incorporation date, jurisdiction of incorporation and registered office address for your company. Then set out the history and development of your company's business for the preceding five years (or less, if your company hasn't been incorporated for that long). If your company has entered into any mergers or reverse-mergers (that's reverse takeovers for our Canadian friends), with other companies, or has suffered any bankruptcy or receiverships, the details must be set out.

Acquisitions and Dispositions—If your company has made any significant asset acquisitions during this five-year period (either for cash, or paid for by issuing stock in your company) then set out full details. "Significant" is a fairly relative term, but you can take it to mean anything that was key to the development of your company, and/or increased the value of your company by 10 percent or more. Similarly, if your company has sold assets over this period, then these details should also be provided.

Business Operations—Set out your company's business operations, including:

- Products and services
- Distribution methods
- Five to seven milestones, which are the main goals your company hopes to accomplish during the next 12 months. These are brief summaries and include the approximate costs to achieve each milestone. Some examples of milestones include:
  - ▷ Complete development of product and service, including first production run of product
  - ▷ Complete development of Website and e-commerce abilities
  - ▷ Establish or expand customer base of [how many] customers
  - ▷ Engage marketing director responsible for implementing marketing plan
  - ▷ Implement facets of marketing program (*i.e.*, attend scheduled trade shows or complete an internet campaign)
  - ▷ Hire additional personnel required by the company to meet milestone expansion targets
- The market for the product/services, including user fees and prices to consumers
- Discuss your company's competition (on an overall industry, specific company and a per-[product/service] basis)
- Status of newly announced and developing products
- Sources and availability of raw materials or principal suppliers

- Customer base, and in particular whether your company is dependent upon a few or certain major customers
- Status of patent and trademark applications
- Whether or not there are any government approval requirements, the effect (if any) of governmental regulations on your company's business, including costs to comply
- Research and development costs (on a per product/service basis for the preceding two years)
- Company's reporting status and current disclosure requirements to shareholders
- Your company's marketing plan for developed products and services and potential marketing plan for products and services in development
  - ▷ include plan for penetration of target market
  - ▷ detail methods (*i.e.* newspaper advertisements, web-advertising, and the like)
  - ▷ set out costs for each marketing phase, including, if new employees are being hired to conduct marketing, and the costs for such employees

Through all of the above, remember to first offer a nice, clear warning that neither you nor your company can guarantee that any of these events will happen at all, but rather these are events that you and your company *hope* will happen. Then liberally salt your discussion with conditional words and phrases such as "expects," "intends," "anticipates," "estimates," "hopes," "may," "wants to," and the like. If you make a statement along the lines of "the company will earn $2.1 million in its first quarter of operations," then your company becomes bound by that statement

—meaning if you don't raise the funds in question your company could be accused of making a material misrepresentation to investors—leading back to potentially nasty consequences. So instead, try "the company intends to implement its marketing plan immediately upon the start of operations and feels that if it is successful in penetrating its target market, first quarter earnings may surpass an estimated $2.1 million."

Management's Discussion and Analysis/Plan of Operations— Much of this information has already been summarily set out earlier in the Business Operations section. This section, to some degree, is a more focused and detailed restatement, where your company describes any existing operational and financial results in addition to management's plan of operations for the next six or twelve months. In this section, you should state whether or not additional funding will be required. Provide a summary of further research and development to be performed and detail anticipated purchases. For each full year of operations you should discuss the company's current financial condition and changes to its financial condition. All discussions should focus specifically on material events and uncertainties known to management. Anything that could impact operations—positive or negative—should be discussed here. Financial projections may also be supplied, along with appropriate disclosure (i.e., whether or not projections were prepared by your company internally or by an accountant and whether the projections have been reviewed by your company's accountant or auditor).

Description of Property—Provide information regarding your company's principal office and other locations, including square footage and ownership status. If leased, set out your company's monthly payments and any other significant terms of the lease. If owned, include mortgage payments and significant terms of the mortgage. If your company has additional manufacturing or warehouse facilities, provide the same information for each facility.

For mining and oil/gas companies, full, extensive disclosure of all mineral and oil/gas properties is also required. Real estate companies must also fully disclose investment policies, investments or interests in real estate, mortgage investments and the types of other businesses in which your company may invest funds.

Employees—List how many full-time and part-time employees you have now and what positions they occupy. Then discuss how many additional employees (and for what positions) will be required during the period following your offering. Advise by how much salaries and wages are expected to increase during this time and from where the funds to pay the additional salaries and wages are going to come.

8. General Miscellaneous Information

Disclosure of Indemnification for Securities Act Liabilities Although your company's bylaws may indemnify its directors and officers, or state law may provide for indemnification, the SEC takes a contrary position, and a statement to this effect is required in all PPMs. There is specific language used for this section that your company's securities attorney can add.

Legal Proceedings—If your company is involved in, or has pending against it, any legal proceedings totaling 10 percent or more of your company's assets, then each claim must be disclosed. The information should include: the court jurisdiction, all parties, a summary of proceedings to date, your company's position, and the relief (amount of claim) sought. However, where the nature of a claim is bankruptcy, receivership or violation of environmental law, your company must make disclosure, regardless of the amount of the claim. Finally, if any of your company's directors, officers, key management personnel or insiders are involved in litigation that could affect your company, you must also provide details.

Risk Factors—This section contains a number of fairly general factors, such as the need for additional financing, lack of an established market, dependence upon key personnel and, if a start-up company, the risks to investors associated with newly emerging companies. Your attorney can supply most of the risk factors. However, where your company has specialized aspects to its operations, it should add in information here, which can be completed by counsel. Examples of company-specific risk factors may be, in our software company example, that your company is subject to possible power interruptions and may suffer data degradation as a result, or that your company may be subject to attack by computer hackers and suffer loss or damage to data. Mining or other natural resource companies may be subject to changing environmental laws that could affect their ability to operate. Natural resource companies with properties in volatile nations may need to add a risk factor stating that political unrest may cause interruption to the ability to manage the property.

The importance of risk factor disclosure cannot be overemphasized. Think of all you can—and then think of more. If any can be cut, your company's attorney can advise you accordingly. It's a lot easier to slice some out rather than rush to include more at the last minute.

A PPM can help your business get the money it needs to grow, but it is a serious undertaking. Be sure to work with the correct professionals to do it right.

Now let's travel abroad with your PPM...

Chapter 18

Regulation S Private Placement Offerings

Do you have connections overseas? You may want to consider a specialized PPM. A Regulation S private placement offering (a "Reg S offering") is similar to conducting a Rule 506 offering, with one key exception—your company is selling only to individuals and companies residing outside of the United States.

There is also one key benefit as well. Unlike a Rule 506 offering, where all investors must be either accredited or sophisticated, and only 35 non-accredited may invest, a Reg S offering has no such limits. Because the sales occur offshore, there are no U.S. investor based requirements, and no limits on the number of investors.

Regulation S of the Securities Act is the legislation under which private or public companies may sell to non-U.S. residents. It is a fairly simple piece of legislation, largely because of the fact that the U.S. government does not consider that it is in the business to look after non-U.S. investors. (How refreshing.) While U.S. securities regulators have written chapter and verse (okay, volumes and volumes) of legislation designed to protect U.S. investors, they are also relying on foreign governments to look after the rights of foreign investors.

To conduct a Reg S offering, a company *should* prepare a PPM along the same lines as a Rule 506 PPM. (While this is not strictly required it is a bad idea not to prepare one.) There are no income or asset tests for investors to meet in offerings made under Reg S, so it is up to you whether or not to provide audited financial statements for your company, although if audited financials exist or were used for a previous Rule 506 offering, it is a very good idea to include them in your Reg S PPM. There is no limit on the number of investors who may subscribe, but again, they must all reside outside of the United States, and they must have no present intent to sell the shares they buy back into the United States.

You may also want to consider that while the U.S. government places no income or asset test restrictions on non-U.S. investors under a Reg S offering, those investors may be subject to some restrictions in their home jurisdiction. As a U.S. company relying on Regulation S, it isn't really your responsibility to check out purchase or investment restrictions in every foreign jurisdiction that your company may sell the offering. But you should make sure that your company's Reg S PPM contains language stating all investors are responsible for making sure that they are allowed to make an investment under the rules of their home jurisdiction. It is also a good idea to make sure that non-U.S. resident investors make a statement to your company that they have complied with securities purchase requirements in their home jurisdiction as well.

When offering stock to foreign investors no directed selling efforts can be made in the United States. Emails and phone calls can be made to those outside the U.S. But the SEC gets concerned when internet Reg S offerings lure in U.S. investors. (If that is your intent use a crowdfunding PPM.) A prominent disclaimer that the offering is only for foreign investors and other safeguards your attorney will suggest should be implemented.

Finally, Regulation S does not appear to pose any restrictions on individuals who may assist your company in selling its offering. Still, you may be well-advised to ask any registered broker-dealers or finders to confirm to your company ahead of time that they are permitted to assist in selling the offering and receiving a commission or a finder's fee.

That sounds easy enough. Let's revisit your software company. As software programmers are a worldwide breed, you have met folks from around the world during the course of your career. You've floated your company's software prototype to a group of friends in Canada, and they all want to invest. You rework your Rule 506 PPM to add in the extra language you need for a Reg S offering, and you're off and running. Your attorney reminds you to make sure that everyone investing can provide some form of proof of residence outside of the United States, and to make sure that your non-U.S. investors don't ask you to have their stock registered in their Nevada asset-holding companies. Because one of the pitfalls of Regulation S is a trail leading back into the United States.

Although U.S. securities regulators and legislators are not overly concerned about stock leaving the country, they are very concerned about that stock coming back in again. In order for Regulation S securities to re-enter the United States they must have been issued for at least one full year, and then may only be resold into the United States under the provisions of the SEC's Rule 144. Stock being resold into the United States will also require a tradability letter confirming that all of the provisions of Reg S have been complied with and that the stock may legitimately come back into the United States.

Rule 144 does not apply to securities sold outside of the United States, which are subsequently resold outside of the

US. In other words, if your company conducts a Reg S offering, the original non US investors may immediately resell all of the securities they purchased—as long as the securities remain outside of the United States. However, while immediate transfers can be done in theory, Regulation S does contain, in the same manner as Regulation D, a proviso that stock being purchased under Regulation S is being purchased for investment rather than for resale, and particularly not for resale into the United States. And, even though the stock may be trading hands on the other side of the U.S. border, the SEC can still conduct investigations into whether a company was attempting to conduct an unregistered public offering through Regulation S. Heck, as a professional courtesy the SEC may even advise the local securities regulators of their investigation and invite them to play along at home. In fact, the SEC keeps their ever-widening eyes on Reg S offerings, because they can be so prone to abuse. Finally, just to make matters more interesting, if the SEC gets wind that your company has conducted a Reg S offering, and then exactly 12 months and three days later the securities your company issued begin to trickle back down into the United States, they can and will come and take a closer look at what your company's underlying intent was when it conducted the Reg S offering.

Being sufficiently cautioned, you ask your attorney how best to make sure your potential investors are all non-U.S. residents and are able to participate in your company's Reg S offering. You and the company must take some precautions, because if the SEC does come looking, you want to be able to show that you have made at least some effort to weed out potentially fraudulent transactions.

When preparing a Regulation S offering it is suggested that all potential investors complete a Declaration of Regulation S Eligibility, in addition to a subscription agreement. (Reg S investors don't need to fill out the Purchaser Suitability Questionnaire because the income/asset test set out in that document doesn't apply.) You may also want to ask for some other proof of residency, such as photocopies of passports and drivers' licenses.

There is a lot of money for investment sitting outside the United States. Go get it.

Now let's provide some cautionary and congratulatory stories to finish it up...

Part Four:
Scams and Successes

Overview

Financing your business is going to be one of the most important activities of your company's existence. It is an ongoing requirement. From start to middle to maturity, you and your company will need to understand and hone the skills of business financing. As such, it is appropriate to conclude with some warnings and some positives. And if you can guide yourself past the scams, you can be one of the success stories, too.

Chapter 19

Scams

Cathy was in desperate need of funds for her business. She was behind on the rent and behind with a few suppliers. Her personal credit was not great, and she didn't really have any business credit lined up. Cathy just knew if she could get a loan and get over the hump that all would be fine. But she needed $8,000 right away and didn't know where to find it.

Then, when she was having her hair done, she saw an ad in one of her favorite tabloids. It read:

Licensed Loan Broker

Easy, fast cash loans from $1,000 to $25,000

No credit/Bad credit OK

Call 877-555-5555

Cathy wrote down the number and went back to work. The first call she made was to the loan broker. The nice person on the other side asked her for some personal and financial information. He asked Cathy to call back in an hour to see if she could qualify for a loan of $8,000.

Cathy was hopeful. On the second call an hour later a 'loan dealer' asked her for more credit history information. He was friendly and encouraging. After several minutes he told Cathy that her loan application had been approved and qualified and that there was very high likelihood that their lenders would successfully obtain a loan for her. Cathy was ecstatic. Her short term money gap would soon be solved.

The nice loan dealer said she needed to submit a written identification and information form, which he would fax her, along with an advance processing fee of $299, payable by money order or a reloadable prepaid card. Both needed to be over-nighted to their address immediately to get the loan funded.

It was hard for Cathy to come up with the $299, but somehow she scraped it together. She was going to get the loan she needed to get over the hump. She overnight mailed the form and money.

Three days later Cathy received a letter saying the loan application had been referred on to the lending organization. The nice loan dealer thanked Cathy for her business.

The next day Cathy received a call from the actual lender, who said all was in order. All they needed was a $99 processing fee to complete the application. Cathy grumbled that she had already paid $299 to the first company. The lender said the loan dealer was an independent company and she had paid their fee. Now, the lender needed $99 for its fee, via a money order delivered to their office in Canada overnight. Cathy re-luctantly agreed. She was so close to the loan she needed.

Three days later Cathy received a letter from the lender stat-ing that they had denied her loan request. She was in shock. She had spent her last $400 on fees for this loan that she desper-ately needed. The nice people had made it seem that the loan was so close, and just a formality. She called the lender for an explanation. She was told her credit was poor. She said they knew that from the start. They hung up. She called again and again. Her calls were never returned.

Distraught, Cathy had no choice but to shut down her business. She was worse off than before. She wished she had never called that toll free number.

As there are many ways to finance your business there are just as many ways for the scam artists of the world to try and separate your money from you. Financing and business credit scams have become more numerous and brazen in recent years. Here are a few to watch out for, since you definitely don't want to be the next victim.

Advance Fee Loans

The advance fee loan scam is alive and well, and perpetuated every day on unsuspecting victims. It has become so prevalent that the Federal Trade Commission (FTC) has issued numerous warnings about it. However, since desperate and vulnerable people are not reading government warnings but rather searching for 'last resort' money to save their business, pay for medical expenses or take care of a funeral, the practice continues unabated.

Here are some tips for not becoming the next victim.

1. Avoid Lenders Who Don't Care About Your Credit. In the real world, loans are based on your creditworthiness. Would you loan money to people with really bad credit? Of course not. So no matter how desperate you are, engage in critical thinking. Step aside from your turmoil for a moment and ask yourself: If my friends, my family, my local bank (and even yourself!) wouldn't loan money to me, why would they? And you will come to the realization that they really don't intend to loan anything to you. They just want the up-front fees. They don't care about putting you further behind than you already are now. They are scamsters. They know you are vulnerable and are playing on that to get at what money you have.

2. Avoid Any Company Asking for Upfront Fees. Legitimate lenders will certainly charge you fees for your loan. The difference is that a legitimate company will deduct these fees from the total amount of the loans provided. You are not paying upfront on the vague hopes of success but rather are paying at the successful conclusion, upon the actual funding of your loan. And so any request for monies for 'processing' or 'insurance' or 'application fees' before a loan is actually granted are the big red flags of a scam.

3. Avoid Firms Asking For Wires, Money Orders or Prepaid Cards. Scammers know that if you use a credit card for a fraudulent service you will have the right to dispute the charge. In such a dispute the charge can be charged back to your card and the money returned to you. (That defeats the whole purpose of the scam!) This is why scamsters insist on money wires, cashier's checks, money orders or prepaid cards. There is no charge back worry with these payments. Your money is gone and so are the scam artists.

4. Avoid Phone Solicitations. It is illegal in the U.S. for companies to call you up to see if you want a loan or a credit card and then ask you to pay for it first. Please just hang up the phone.

5. Investigate Firms with Even the Most Respected Names. Scamsters are great at creating company names that appear respected and well known. Some names are blatant copies of well-known banks, others are just a shade off. For example, there is a well-known credit union in California named 'Golden 1.' Scam artists have used the name 'Golden One' to mislead victims. They will set up professional looking websites and provide you with fake personal references. Double check everything. Call directory assistance for their phone number and call to check up on them. Visit their offices if you can. If they use a P.O. Box and can't provide a legitimate street address, run from them.

6. Make Sure the Company is Registered in Your State. All lenders and loan brokers must be licensed to do business in the states they lend in. Go online or call your state's Attorney General's office or Department of Banking to check on their registration. If they aren't registered you are dealing with a scam artist.

7. Beware of Foreign Lenders. Just as lenders must be registered in your state they should be doing business in your home county. With all due respect to our Canadian readers, Americans should never send loan fees up to Canada. Dozens of bucket shop scam companies have set up in Canada. The reasons are twofold. First, the penalties in Canada are very light, if one ever does get caught. A typical sentence is 60 days, as the Canadians treat these matters as a minor consumer dispute. In Texas, on the other hand, such activities are viewed as fraud and can come with a 15 year prison term. So you can see why the scamsters are in Canada. Don't send your money there. The second issue is related to the state issue. These foreign firms aren't licensed to do business in your home country. No license, no legitimate loans.

8. Avoid Firms Misrepresenting SBA Loans. The Small Business Administration (SBA) has issued warnings about scamsters misrepresenting themselves as preferred companies for SBA loans. For a high fee, the scamsters will 'guarantee' you an SBA loan. If you don't use their service they will threaten to send you a 'forfeiture' letter alleging that you are barred from applying for an SBA loan for three or more years. The SBA asserts that they never make guarantees of loans (again, such loans are based on your creditworthiness) and there is no such thing as a forfeiture letter. The irony is that the SBA's services are free. (Visit www.sba.gov or call 1-800-827-5722). A cardinal rule: Never pay a scamster for what you can get for free.

Equipment Lease Ripoffs

Equipment leases come with fine print. If you don't read the fine print you can get scammed when you try to lease your next copier, vehicle or other piece of equipment. Here are some tips when it comes to leasing:

1. **Watch Out for Companies Asking for a Deposit Before the Lease is Approved**. Like the advance fee loan scam, many unscrupulous leasing companies make their money by requiring a deposit and then, when underwriter approval is denied, failing to return the money. While a small credit check and/or application fee is not unusual, asking for an advance payment before the deal is finalized most certainly is.

2. **Only Work With Companies Belonging to Legitimate Leasing Organizations**. Visit the leasing company's website (they must have a website!) and check if they belong to a leasing association. If they don't, walk away. If they do, double check it. Many scamsters misuse logos to deceive. Actually call the association to make sure the company is in good standing and does not have a history of complaints.

3. **Have your Attorney Review the Contract**. Is it better to spend a few hundred dollars now to save ten thousand dollars later? It is your call. But as Robert Kiyosaki says, "Business is a team sport." This is a good time to use the attorney on your team to review the lease.

4. **Avoid Any Lease with an Evergreen Clause**. This one actually happened to me. We were going to lease a copier from a big, well known Fortune 500 company. I certainly thought they were reputable. I was on the road and our staff said we really needed the copier right away. Big mistake. Never be rushed, by anyone. The lease contained a clause with a $1 buy out at the end of the term. But if you didn't exercise the buyout by giving them notice the company would, with no duty

to notify you, just continue to accept the automatic electronic monthly payments. It was an 'evergreen lease' that would go on forever. We paid an extra year on the copier before we discovered the mistake. When we demanded our money back the large reputable company was just as nasty and greedy as a scam artist. I lost a lot of faith in the ethics of big American business operations from this incident. Basically, you can't trust anyone.

5. If You Are a Reputable Lessor, Beware of Scam Lessees. For as many scam leasing companies as there are there are just as many dishonest lessees. These are the criminals who induce lessors, or the provider of any product or service, to enter into an equipment lease. They then disappear with the goods and never make a payment. Some signs to look for:

- Numerous trade references that are too good to be true.
- Excellent financials provided when not requested.
- A need for a rush approval (always a red flag in any situation).
- A last minute change in the 'ship to' address. Scamsters will use real credit information from established companies, including a correct street address. Right before shipping they will request it directed to a 'satellite office.'

As the large equipment finance companies know, small customers and small equipment can very easily vanish.

More Scams

There are a multitude of other scams in the marketplace. You must engage in critical thinking at all times. While we cannot cover all of them here, we present a few more as a warning of what is out there.

File Segregation

Consumers with a bad credit history are encouraged by credit repair companies to apply for a new taxpayer identification or employer identification number. The idea is to use these new numbers to hide their true credit identity from creditors. Essentially, you are segregating your old credit file from your 'new' credit file. The only problem is that under the law this is a felony, meaning at least a year in jail if you are caught. Run from the company that suggests file segregation.

Toner Phoner

This office supply scam works best on harried receptionists who juggle phones, customers and a variety of both routine and unusual tasks all day long. The caller identifies themselves by first name, as if you are already familiar with who they are, and asks for the serial number of your copier. If you give them the information, you will soon receive an invoice for toner (paper or other office supplies) at greatly inflated prices. You may even receive inferior toner or paper too. Many companies pay for the supplies, not realizing they never actually ordered it in the first place.

As this scam has been around for decades, most office staff are now wise to it. Receptionists have learned not to give out identifying information on their office equipment. Keep in mind, your regular supplier will already know what equipment you have and supplies you order. If you happen to get a caller who asks you for your copier information, simply ask the caller to identify what company they work for. The response will vary from a simple hang-up, to the caller becoming belligerent or even cursing at you, all good indicators that this is a scam. Just hang up.

Phony Invoices

Like the telephone calls you will get, you will also receive phony invoices through the mail. These are mass mailed on the theory that a certain percentage will be mindlessly paid. And the theory works in practice. Many bookkeepers are tricked into paying what is not actually an invoice for a service that will never be provided. Have you ever received an invoice for what looks to be from the Yellow Pages? When you inspect it you realize you never ordered such an ad and you toss the invoice. Know that not everyone tosses it, and that enough get paid to keep the scam alive.

Prime Bank Schemes

Of all the scams out there this is the one that sucks in the most sophisticated people. While there are a number of variations, the promoters (who of course receive an upfront fee) basically state that risk free, triple digit returns can be had on debt notes guaranteed by the world's biggest banks. These notes can then be used to finance worthy businesses as part of a grand scheme by the world's central banks to recycle money around the globe. I have had clients put their lives on hold waiting for the big money to arrive. The problem is there is always an excuse for why the funding is held up. ("The bank in France won't release it yet." "We need another notarized signature." "The affiliated charity officer was sick last week.") When I warn clients that I have never seen one of these transactions ever be funded they will scoff and suggest that I am not attuned to how the real world of big money operates. And surprisingly, after three years of waiting for the money to arrive, these people will assume it was just their big deal that was not funded. Despite all evidence to the contrary, they are still strangely convinced that these shadowy multinational transactions really do occur. Which is their right. You can also believe in Bigfoot if you want.

Small Business ID Theft

As if small business owners don't have enough to deal with, small business ID theft is a growing risk. In fact, small business owners are one-and-a-half times more likely to be a victim than other adults, according to a recent Javelin Strategy & Research Identity Fraud Survey Report, cosponsored by the Identity Theft Assistance Center. Some of this fraud is committed by insiders; employees who have access to company information. But it is also very easy for scammers to impersonate a business. They may purchase equipment and supplies using the small business's identity and then resell the items they bought. Or they may drain the victim's bank account. Unfortunately, this is an easy crime to commit. It is hard for business owners to catch and since many don't monitor their business credit, it can go undetected for quite a while. You may seriously want to consider monitoring your business and personal credit to catch suspicious activity as quickly as possible. See the Resource Section for suggestions.

Cyber Crooks

Has an employee ever left a laptop behind at a conference? Has anyone in your company (including you) ever had a smartphone stolen or misplaced?

The resulting hassle involves two tasks. The first one many have experienced—getting a new phone or laptop, replacing contact information, accessing duplicate work documents and the like.

The second task involves much larger issues. What if your electronics hold private information on clients and employees, and passwords for your business? You have a lot more to deal with in such a case.

Worse yet, imagine that your company has come under attack by a skilled hacker who has accessed your customer and employee's personal information—names, contact info, even social security numbers—from your company's database. What if your website is disabled and you cannot take orders or collect the payments you need to stay in business? This happens to companies, large and small, every day and the costs are enormous. While we all know that losing a tablet or phone is more common than having your server hacked, both happen too often to dismiss.

Cyber liability coverage is insurance coverage for the liability that arises out of the unauthorized use of, or access to, electronic data or software within your network or business. Cyber liability policies also provide coverage for liability claims for spreading malicious code or viruses, computer theft, extortion, or any unintentional act, mistake, error or omission made by an employee while doing their job.

Traditional business insurance policies usually only cover "tangible" assets. Electronic data is not considered tangible under the typical insurance definition.

This means that while a normal commercial insurance policy may cover the loss of the equipment, for the losses associated with compromised personal and private information you may need a "cyber liability" insurance policy. Know that the financial exposure from a breach can be significant.

How can a cyber-liability policy cover you? Here are some ways:

- You may be sued for the information breach. A cyber policy can cover the legal fees and insurance involved.
- You will have to notify clients and employees of the breach. The notification fees can be satisfied by the policy.
- If your website is hacked and shut down the lost income from a lack of sales can be covered.
- If you have to hire a public relations firm to regain your standing such fees can be paid by the policy.

One more thing to note is that even if you don't host your data yourself, you are still responsible. Is your website or any of your data hosted or stored in "the cloud"? If so, you are still legally responsible. Since you can't fully control how a cloud provider handles your data, a cyber-liability policy can protect you if your cloud provider fails to do so.

The Department of Commerce Internet Policy Task Force has described cyber liability insurance as a means of encouraging the implementation of best practices by basing premiums on an insured's level of self-protection, and thus limiting the level of losses that companies face following a cyber-attack.

This is not a policy for just large businesses. The notice and remediation requirements apply to small firms as well. Premiums are affordable and start at approximately $1,000 per year. Meet with your insurance professional and go through the risks involved. Know that insurance companies may encourage and assist with risk-management strategies. Of course, the more careful and protected you are the better it is for the insurance company. They will be on your side to protect their pay out rates.

All businesses, large and small, are subject to cyber liability claims. While a corporation and/or LLC will offer asset protection, a cyber-liability insurance policy will help cover those risky, out of the blue claims that can challenge your business' assets and operational future.

As a preventative measure before there is a problem, you may also want to consider obtaining fidelity insurance. You probably have insurance for fire and property damage. Why not get insurance to protect you from fraud and embezzlement? It may be as easy as adding a fidelity rider to your existing policy. Talk to your insurance agent about whether fidelity insurance makes sense for you.

What To Do If You've Been Scammed.

With all the challenges out there it is important to know what to do if you are a victim. Don't be silent and don't be embarrassed. Speak up. You may help save the next potential victim from trouble. Report the crime to your local police department. They probably won't help you get your money back but for insurance and income tax purposes you'll need to have filed a police report. You should also report it to your state attorney general's office, which can be found at: www.naag.org/current-attorneys-general.php. For U.S. citizens you can also report problems to the Federal Trade Commission at: www.ftc.gov or call toll free 1-877-382-4357. In Canada, the link for reporting is www.recol.ca. In the UK, the ConsumerDirect website is secure.consumer-direct.gov.uk/reportascam.aspx. Other countries have similar links for reporting.

All right, enough warnings. It is time for some successes…

Chapter 20

Putting It All Together

Starting and running a small business can be a series of ups and downs, steps forward and backward. Sometimes you will feel like you are losing ground. But there's a saying for that: "What doesn't kill you makes you stronger." In the case of entrepreneurs, what doesn't kill your business can make it stronger.

If At First You Don't Succeed

For the past decade, California Cycleworks has been building a loyal following selling aftermarket parts for motorcycles, including parts for top of the line Italian Ducati bikes. Over the years, owner Chris Kelley has developed a feel for what his customers want. But he's not willing to bet his business on his gut. "Many people talk about what they want but when it comes time to actually pay up, many bail out," says Kelley.

So instead, he's turned to crowdfunding—even before the word existed. Here is Chris Kelley's story in his words:

"Our first product from crowdfunding was a 'group buy/preorder' list on an enthusiast forum in 2006 for me to make a larger capacity fuel tank for the Ducati MH900e. It was financially backed by my ex-wife until we got the 30-plus initial orders shipped and could start paying her back. It was her bike that went to the R&D facility for the design.

"A few years later, one of my best customers convinced me to do a large tank for the Hypermotard 1100 and used my first model as the basis to start a list on another forum.

"Was it coincidence that my ex-wife owned one of these bikes as well? Or providence?

"This time, the big 2008 crash had happened and I was leery of taking on a huge project. That customer herded the cats for us and when we got 60+ people on our buy in list, we started the project and began taking pre-orders and customers' money via credit cards. My ex-wife's new bike went under the knife at a new R&D shop. When it came time to ship the product, only half of the people who promised to buy actually bought. We got lucky and managed to squeak by.

"That same Hypermotard model crowd wanted another version of the tank with less capacity. They didn't like that I made the fuel tank too big! Eventually, I did the R&D, started a list, but then realized I could let crowdfunding be the judge. The funding site everyone knows declined my project and gave us zero help getting it approved. My assumption is we aren't video artists and our presentation wasn't polished enough. So we turned to another crowdfunding site. I had the feeling this crowd wasn't going to actually come through—and they didn't.

"For our recent successful project—the Multistrada fuel tank—I didn't want to use the site we had just tried because they did not have an 'all or nothing' option. And when the folks couldn't come through to actually get that project working, it ended up costing us a few thousand dollars, for a project we wouldn't even start.

"We searched and found Invested.in with its choices of campaign end-game options. I liked it and decided to go for it. I used one of the complaints from the previous failed campaign that the period was too short so I made the Multistrada tank funding project 60 days instead of 30. I'm just glad we got accepted so we wouldn't have to waste a week-plus making spiffy videos and begging that other platform for project approval.

"Ultimately, we implored our interested customers to spread the word everywhere they could. An enthusiast forum thread was again the foundation for the project and the primary source of investors.

"We were successful this time because we had a number of exceptionally passionate customers. Some bought multiple articles. Others asked us to come up with a way to simply loan us money, so we came up with a few lending tiers. Also, we set the time limit to 60 days. I feel from here on, that should be the minimum time frame and 90 or 120 days is more realistic."

Like many entrepreneurs, Kelley has used other sources of financing as well. Again, in his words:

"My business secured a line of credit with the bank where we have our checking account. When the big slump of 2008 hit, I maxed it out trying to keep the business running. I came close to seeking work as a programmer again to fund my employees' salary and pay rent, but the line of credit and all the other ways I could raise money kept us open. Since I have that huge debt, I haven't sought loans since.

"My ex-wife is still an active investor but I try to limit my dependence on her for money. If there comes a time when I really need it, I'm saving her for those. She believes in my vision and is active in my business practice and I'm very thankful!

"A friend from college is another possible source of investment. She has capital but cannot make any income on it now that banks are only offering interest under 1%. Here, too, I value my relationship more than getting money from it, so I'm hesitant."

Kelley offers several tips for entrepreneurs considering crowdfunding:

1) Just do it. And if the project doesn't get approved or enough investors, keep at it. The 'all or nothing' model is the way to go. If you don't get enough money, you're not on the hook.

2) Plan at least a week of work to get the project set up before trying to launch it. Look at successfully funded projects on the same site or others for inspiration. If you have the capacity to make a slick and polished music video for your dream, then go for it. If you're a normal outfit like ours, do the best you can. The web interface at Invested.in is very friendly; the best of the three crowdfunding sites I have used.

3) Ask for at least 30% more than you think you need. Or more. I have completed dozens of projects for $10,000 or more and none of them come in on budget. Something always needs a change or there is a detail hiding behind the scenes to derail your efforts. Perhaps freight is more than you thought (or just plain impossible!)

Many more successful stories will come from crowdfunding. You can be a part of it.

You Can Start Again

In 2008, Robin Bramman opened a boutique in a shopping center that became the largest commercial foreclosure in the state of Arizona. As the local and national economy went into meltdown, it took her business with it. "I had to file a business and personal bankruptcy," she says.

But Robin has an entrepreneurial spirit and wouldn't let one failure stop her in her tracks. She was connected to a business credit coach who helped her start over again.

She's come a long way in a relatively short period of time. "When we started (in 2010), my personal credit was in the low 600s. I checked it recently and it is in the low 700s. I have already established a Paydex score," she says.

Three years later, she has a thriving business focused on branding and social media on the web. "I didn't want to do bricks and mortar anymore," she says.

Before going back into full-time entrepreneurial work she held a consulting job and worked part time. Her spouse was also working so she was able to put all of her earnings back into the business to keep it fully self-funded.

But she realizes how important business credit is so she has a gas card, a business credit card, a business checking account and an online office supply store account.

Her credit lines are increasing, and she buys all her office supplies online to help build her business credit rating. She is also looking into getting her next vehicle through the business.

She's very mindful of cash flow, and has clients on retainer rather than on service-based fees. She says she's much more careful about her spending.

"We are in the process of buying a home again so we have completely reestablished our business and personal credit," she observes. "We live lean but comfortably."

Another key to her success, she says is her "trifecta power team" of advisors, which is made up of her CPA, attorney, and her credit coach whom she talks with before making an important decision. "Always look to your power team."

As Robin's business grows, she expects to keep building her business credit along with it.

"Zero personal guarantees. That's my goal now."

Conclusion

Entrepreneurs and investors get funded every day. It is not always easy. It is not always fun. But it can be done.

Bill Rasmussen, the founder of ESPN, faced numerous funding challenges and roadblocks on his way to build an iconic global business. Bill persevered and never lost an ounce of enthusiasm for his project. His success in launching ESPN was hard fought and enduring. You too can follow this path—you have learned the strategies and sources for business financing. Apply your dedication, energies and resolve and you will find the financing solution that is right for you. Again, it can be done.

But you don't have to do it alone.

We want to help! At CorporateDirect.com, you'll find additional resources to help you implement the strategies we've described here. You can get updates to this material as well as learn even more from the experts featured. We hope you'll continue your journey there with us.

Best wishes in all your endeavors.

Appendix A

Due Diligence Checklist

A financing transaction may require the review of some or all of the items listed below. Of course, some documents may not be available for newer companies as specific events have not yet taken place. *Please also know that this list is very comprehensive. Your transaction may not require this level of information.*

All references to the Company include all predecessor and subsidiary corporations.

****

General Corporate Documents

Business Plan

Minutes

- Minutes of stockholders' meetings
- Minutes of board of directors' meetings
- Minutes of permanent committees of the board
- Authorizing resolutions relating to the financing and related transactions

Charter Documents

- Articles of Incorporation, as amended to date
- Bylaws, as amended to date
- Good standing (and franchise tax board) certificates
- List of jurisdictions in which the Company (or any of its subsidiaries or affiliates) is qualified to do business

Corporate Organization

- List of officers and directors
- Management structure organization chart
- Stockholders' lists, including number of shares and dates of issuance, and consideration paid
- Information regarding subsidiaries, i.e., ownership, date of acquisition of stock and/or assets, all closing binders relating to acquisitions
- Information regarding joint ventures or partnership, i.e., partners, date of formation and all closing binders relating to joint ventures or partnerships

Capital Stock

- Stock records, stock ledgers and other evidence of securities authorized and issued
- Agreements relating to registration rights and preemptive or other preferential rights to acquire securities
- Agreements relating to voting of securities and restrictive share transfers
- Evidence of qualification or exemption under applicable federal and state blue sky laws for issuance of the Company's securities

Compliance with Laws

- Any citations and notices received from government agencies
- Any pending or threatened investigations and governmental proceedings
- All material governmental permits, licenses, etc. of the Company presently in force as well as information regarding any such permits, licenses, etc., which have been cancelled or terminated
- All documents filed with the SEC or any state or foreign securities regulatory agency, if any

- Any material reports to and correspondence with any government entity, municipality or government agency, including the EPA and OSHA

Litigation

- Any litigation, claims, and proceedings settled or concluded
- Any litigation, claims, and proceedings threatened or pending
- Any consent decrees, settlement agreements, judgments or other decrees or orders
- Any litigation involving an executive officer or director, including executive officers or directors of predecessor corporations and subsidiaries, concerning bankruptcy, crimes, securities law or business practices
- All attorneys' letters to auditors

Employee Matters

- Employee agreements
- Consulting contracts
- Employee benefit and profit-sharing plans, including stock option, stock purchase, deferred compensation, and bonus plans or arrangements
- All other employee compensation, incentive, retirement, benefit or similar plans, including compliance with federal laws regarding health insurance
- Employee Confidentiality and/or Proprietary Rights Agreement
- Contracts with unions and other labor agreements
- Loans to and guarantees for the benefit of directors, officers or employees.
- "Key person" insurance policies
- Listing of employees by office and department

Management Team

- What is the caliber/pedigree of the team?
- What is the team's overall track record?
- Do they have the combined requisite skills and experience?
- Do they recognize limitations in management, and are they seeking candidates?
- Is the management open to discussion and suggestions on improvement to their business model?
- Has the management team been previously funded?
- How are management and all other employees being compensated?
- Does the Company have an option plan, and have options been granted to all employees? What percentage do the founders have as compared to other key management?
- What is the stock ownership of directors and of the five most-highly compensated officers?

Real Property

- Deeds
- Leases of real property
- Other interests in real property
- Financing leases and sale and lease-back agreements
- Conditional sale agreements
- Equipment leases

Intellectual Property Matters

- List of all domestic and foreign patents, patent applications, copyrights, patent licenses and copyright licenses held by the Company

- List of any trademarks, trademark applications, trade names, or service marks
- Infringement or misappropriation notices or demands of others' patents, copyrights, trademarks, trade secrets or other proprietary rights
- Copies of all licensing and distribution agreements for any technology, including without limitation software licenses, patent licenses, or other technology licenses, any development or joint-development agreements, or any OEM, VAR or sales representative agreements

Technology Assessment

(May need expert or professional assistance in Technology Assessment to perform this.)

- Do they have market requirements and functional specifications?
- At what stage is development? Concept, alpha, beta, shipping?
- Does the Company have any usability studies?
- Does the Company have adequate intellectual-property protection? Does it need it?
- Is the Company relying on being first to market, rather than on any IP position, for competitive advantage, and is this realistic?
- What is product quality assurance like?
- Has the Company properly set up relationships and documentation to ensure ownership of all intellectual property?
- Does the Company own all necessary intellectual property through internal development or licenses?
- Do any other Companies have potential claims to the IP resulting from previous employment relationships or for any other reason?

Operations

- Operating plan or outline if early stage
- For mature companies, the operating plan for each division
- Any plans showing the Company has considered all aspects of operation to successfully launch a product or service
- Any plans for anticipated growth
- Any citations or notices of violation the Company has received
- All material correspondence about management meetings to ensure compliance with plan and any adjustments made
- Cash needs and anticipated cash flow
- Plans and alternative plans for product rollout, and market response

Debt Financing

- All Debt instruments, credit agreements, and guarantees entered into by the Company, including lease financing, which are currently in effect
- All material correspondence with lenders, including all compliance reports submitted by the Company or its accountants
- Any loans and guarantees of third-party obligations
- Any agreements restricting the payment of cash dividends

Financial Information

- Audited/unaudited financial statements, including those of any predecessor corporations
- Interim financial statements
- Budget plan, including revisions to date with respect to the budget plan for the current fiscal year for the Company
- The Company's long-range strategic plan, any other doc-

uments concerning its long-range plans, and any information concerning the Company's compliance therewith

•Disclosure documents used in private placements of the Company's or any of its subsidiaries' or affiliates' securities, or institutional, or bank loan applications since inception

•Any other material agreements with creditors

•Significant correspondence with independent public accountants, including management letters

•Any reports, studies and projections prepared by management on the Company's business, financial condition, or planned operations, including the business plan

•Any reports and studies prepared by outside consultants on the Company's business or financial condition

•Reports and materials prepared for the Company's board of directors or a committee thereof

•Contracts with investment bankers and brokers

Tax Matters

•Federal, state and local tax returns, including those of any predecessor corporations

•Any audit adjustments proposed by the IRS

•Any tax compliance correspondence

Acquisitions/Divestitures

•Acquisitions or divestitures (including related documentation)

•Current plans or negotiations relating to potential acquisitions or divestitures

Other Agreements

•Marketing agreements

•Management and service agreements

• Confidentiality, and non-disclosure agreements
• Agreements restricting the Company's right to compete or other agreements material to the business
• Contracts outside the ordinary course of business
• Agreements requiring consents or approvals with change-of-control transactions
• Indemnification contracts and similar arrangements for officers and directors
• Agreements with officers, directors and affiliated parties
• Agreements with competitors
• Agreements with governmental agencies or institutions
• Material insurance agreements (including property damage, third-party liability and key employee insurance)

Public Relations

• Annual reports and other reports and communications with stockholders, employees, suppliers and customers
• Advertising, marketing and other selling materials

Press Releases and Clippings

• Press reports as published
• Wire releases
• Analyst reports

Miscellaneous

• Copies of all market research and/or studies concerning the Company's business
• Significant agreements currently in draft stage

Appendix B:

Private Placement Memorandum Template

The private placement memorandum (PPM) found in this Appendix, and the real estate risk factors found in Appendix C, are only templates for your illustration and review. They must not be used without the receipt of appropriate legal advice and counsel from a securities attorney.

Violation of the securities laws come with both civil and criminal penalties. You must absolutely work with a securities attorney when venturing into this area.

A fundamental principle in preparing a PPM is complete disclosure so that a potential investor can make a reasonable and informed investment decision. Of course, this template does not fit every situation and without editing and scrutiny will not serve as a suitable investment document.

The terms in this PPM (interest offered, price per interest and the like) are fictional and provided solely for the purpose of an example. You and your advisors must develop and utilize term suited to your specific needs. Alright, enough warnings. You get the picture.

No. _____

AWESOME COMPANY, LLC

A Nevada Limited Liability Company

CONFIDENTIAL PRIVATE PLACEMENT
MEMORANDUM

Dated: _____, 20__

Offering: A maximum of 400,000 membership interests (the "Interests"), sold in units consisting of 25,000 interests per unit (the "Units"). A total of 16 Units will be sold, with the per-Unit purchase price of $50,000. Gross proceeds to be raised will be approximately $800,000.

Minimum Purchase: 1 Unit of 25,000 Interests (or $50,000)

Awesome Company, LLC., ("we," or "us") is a development-stage Nevada Limited Liability Company formed to develop and operate a _____ in _____. We will _____. We are seeking to raise $800,000 from investors to commence our operations.

Offers to subscribe under the Offering will only be made to those persons or entities that meet our minimum net worth and/or income qualifications and standards. The Offering will commence on_____, 20__, and will expire on_____, 20__, unless extended (the "Offering Period"). If we sell all of the Units before_____, 20__, we will close the Offering before that date.

You must purchase a minimum of one Unit of 25,000 Interests, for a minimum investment amount of $50,000. However we may, in our sole discretion, accept subscriptions for lesser amounts.

	Individual Subscription	Commissions	Proceeds to Company
Per-Investor Purchase	$50,000	$0	$50,000
Aggregate Purchase	$800,000	$0	$800,000

1) We intend to sell the Units primarily through the efforts of our officers, directors and senior management. These individuals will not receive any commissions in connection with their efforts on our behalf.

2) Expenses of the Offering are discussed under "USE OF PROCEEDS."

THESE ARE SPECULATIVE SECURITIES AND INVOLVE A NUMBER OF SUBSTANTIAL RISKS. SEE "RISK FACTORS"

PURCHASE OF THESE SECURITIES INVOLVES A HIGH DEGREE OF RISK.

THE UNITS OFFERED PURSUANT TO THIS PRIVATE PLACEMENT MEMORANDUM ("MEMORANDUM") HAVE NOT BEEN REGISTERED WITH OR APPROVED OR DISAPPROVED BY THE SECURITIES AND EXCHANGE COMMISSION, THE STATE SECURITIES COMMISSION FOR NEVADA OR ANY OTHER STATE SECURITIES COMMISSION AND NO COMMISSIONS OR ADMINISTRATORS HAVE PASSED UPON THE ACCURACY OR ADEQUACY OF THIS MEMORANDUM. ANY REPRESENTATION TO THE CONTRARY IS A CRIMINAL OFFENSE.

THIS MEMORANDUM IS NOT AN OFFER TO SELL UNITS TO YOU OR A PROMISE BY YOU TO PURCHASE UNITS FROM US. WHEN YOU SUBMIT YOUR SUBSCRIPTION DOCUMENTATION WE WILL DETERMINE (IN OUR SOLE DISCRETION) THAT YOU MEET OUR INVESTOR QUALIFICATIONS. ALL INVESTORS WILL BE REQUIRED TO MAKE REPRESENTATIONS TO US THAT INCLUDE YOUR INVESTMENT INTENT, DEGREE OF SOPHISTICATION, ACCESS TO INFORMATION CONCERNING US AND YOUR ABILITY TO BEAR THE ECONOMIC RISK OF THE INVESTMENT.

IF YOU DO NOT MEET OUR INVESTOR QUALIFICATIONS, THIS INVESTMENT IS UNSUITABLE FOR YOU. THESE UNITS ARE SUITABLE ONLY FOR INVESTORS WHO HAVE SUBSTANTIAL FINANCIAL RESOURCES AND HAVE NO NEED FOR LIQUIDITY IN THIS INVESTMENT. YOU SHOULD NOT INVEST IN US IF YOU CANNOT AFFORD TO LOSE YOUR ENTIRE INVESTMENT. YOU SHOULD CAREFULLY CONSIDER THE RISK FACTORS SET OUT IN THE MEMORANDUM UNDER THE HEADING, "RISK FACTORS".

BECAUSE WE ARE SELLING THE UNITS AS UNREGISTERED SECURITIES, WE ARE RELYING ON CERTAIN REGISTRATION EXEMPTIONS AVAILABLE UNDER THE *SECURITIES ACT OF 1933,* AS AMENDED

(THE "SECURITIES ACT"), AND STATE SECURITIES LAWS FOR SALES OF SECURITIES THAT DO NOT INVOLVE MAKING A PUBLIC OFFERING. THIS MEMORANDUM DOES NOT CONSTITUTE AN OFFER OR SOLICITATION IN ANY JURISDICTION WHERE SUCH AN OFFER OR SOLICITATION WOULD BE UNLAWFUL.

THE CONTENTS OF THIS MEMORANDUM AND ANY OTHER COMMUNICATION, WRITTEN OR ORAL, THAT YOU RECEIVE FROM US OR ANY OF OUR AGENTS MAY NOT BE CONSIDERED AS LEGAL, TAX, ACCOUNTING OR OTHER EXPERT ADVICE. YOU MUST CONSULT YOUR OWN COUNSEL, ACCOUNTANT AND PROFESSIONAL ADVISORS AS TO WHETHER INVESTING IN US IS SUITABLE FOR YOU AND ANY LEGAL, TAX, ACCOUNTING OR RELATED MATTERS THAT MAY ARISE. YOU MUST RELY ON YOUR OWN EXAMINATION OF US AND THE TERMS OF THE OFFERING, INCLUDING THE MERITS AND RISKS INVOLVED IN DECIDING TO INVEST IN US.

YOU MAY ONLY RELY ON THE ACCURACY OF INFORMATION THAT IS PRESENTED IN THIS MEMORANDUM OR THAT IS PROVIDED DIRECTLY TO YOU BY OUR AUTHORIZED REPRESENTATIVE(S). YOU SHOULD NOT RELY ON ANY OTHER INFORMATION AS IT MAY BE UNAUTHORIZED AND INCORRECT. IF YOU WANT MORE INFORMATION THAN THAT CONTAINED IN THIS MEMORANDUM, YOU MAY CONTACT _____ at _____.

THE UNITS YOU PURCHASE WILL BE SUBJECT TO RESTRICTIONS ON TRANSFERABILITY AND RESALE AND MAY NOT BE TRANSFERRED OR RESOLD EXCEPT AS ALLOWED UNDER THE SECURITIES ACT. YOU SHOULD BE AWARE THAT YOU MAY BE REQUIRED TO BEAR THE FINANCIAL RISKS OF YOUR INVESTMENT IN US FOR AN INDEFINITE PERIOD OF TIME.

ALL SHARE CERTIFICATES PRINTED WILL HAVE THE FOLLOWING LEGEND PRINTED ON THEM:
THE SECURITIES OFFERED HEREBY HAVE NOT BEEN REGISTERED UNDER THE <u>SECURITIES ACT OF 1933</u>, AS AMENDED (THE "SECURITIES ACT"), OR ANY STATE SECURITIES LAWS. THE SECURITIES REPRESENTED BY THIS CERTIFICATE HAVE BEEN ACQUIRED FOR INVESTMENT, AND NOT WITH A VIEW TO, OR IN CONNECTION WITH, THE SALE OR DISPOSITION

THEREOF. NO SUCH SALE OR DISPOSITION MAY BE MADE WITHOUT (1) AN EFFECTIVE REGISTRATION STATEMENT RELATING THERETO, OR AN OPINION OF COUNSEL (SATIS-FACTORY TO THE COMPANY) THAT SUCH REGISTRATION IS NOT REQUIRED UNDER THE SECURITIES ACT; AND (2) IN COMPLIANCE WITH ANY APPLICABLE STATE SECURITIES LAWS.

YOU MAY NOT COPY THIS MEMORANDUM OR GIVE IT ANYONE ELSE. BY ACCEPTING DELIVERY OF THIS MEMORANDUM, YOU AGREE TO RETURN IT PROMPTLY TO US (TOGETHER WITH ANY OTHER DOCUMENTS OR WRITTEN INFORMATION WE PROVIDE TO YOU) IF YOU DECIDE NOT TO PURCHASE ANY UNITS.

TABLE OF CONTENTS

This Private Placement Memorandum is composed of the Sections specified below.

SUMMARY

The following summary is qualified in its entirety by detailed information appearing elsewhere in this Private Placement Memorandum:

The Company	Awesome, LLC, a Nevada Limited Liability Company, formed on _____, 20___.
The Business	We are a development-stage company that has been formed to develop and operate a _____ in _____. See "DESCRIPTION OF THE COMPANY."
Securities Offered	Membership interests (the "Interests") being sold in units (the "Units"). Each Unit consists of 25,000 Interests. A total of 16 Units are being offered for sale. See "Interests Being Offered."
Price per Unit/ Price per Interest	$50,000 per Unit, or $2.00 per Share There is a minimum purchase requirement of one Unit, for a minimum dollar investment amount of $50,000. We reserve the right, in our sole discretion, to waive this minimum purchase requirement. All purchases must be made in cash. See "Investor Suitability Standards" to determine whether or not you are qualified to invest in us under the Offering. We are under no obligation to accept your subscription agreement, and we may, in our sole discretion, accept or reject your subscription agreement regardless of whether or not you meet our investor qualifications. We may accept subscription agreements to purchase any amount of Units.
Offering Expiration Date	The earlier of: (a) the sale of all Units offered; (b) _____, 20__, subject to our option, in our sole discretion, to extend the Offering up to_____, 20__; or (c) at any time, upon our decision, in our sole discretion, to terminate the Offering.
Investor Suitability	The Units being offered are being sold as unregistered securities. The Offering is available to Accredited investors, Purchaser Representative-Assisted investors and Non-Accredited investors under an exemption found in Regulation D, Rule 506. See "Investor Suitability Standards" for a definition of Accredited, Purchaser Representative-Assisted and Non-Accredited investors. See "Investor Suitability Standards." See also "Plan of Distribution" for a more detailed discussion of our share capital structure.

Plan of Distribution	The Units described in this Private Placement Memorandum are being sold under Rule 506 of Regulation D of the Securities Act, 1933, as amended (the "Securities Act"). We may offer the Units in such states or non-US jurisdictions as we may decide, in our sole discretion, subject to meeting the regulatory filing requirements for each such state and non-US jurisdiction in which Units are sold. We intend to sell the Units primarily through the efforts of our directors, officers, senior management and other authorized representatives. No commissions shall be payable to any of these individuals in connection with any sales of the Units. There will be no general solicitation of investors.
Use of Proceeds	We intend to use the proceeds of the Offering to acquire equipment for working capital and to commence active operations. See "Use of Proceeds." **There will be no escrow of purchase funds received from the sale of Units and we will be entitled to use all monies received from any subscriber immediately.**
LLC Restrictions and Compliance	We are defined by the Internal Revenue Service as a flow thorough tax entity. That means that we are taxed differently than a regular corporation. Our net profits and losses will flow through to you and you will be required to report your portion on your personal tax return and to pay the taxes on that amount. See "Investor Suitability Standards."

RISK FACTORS

The securities offered herein are speculative and involve a number of significant risks. You should carefully consider the following risk factors before making an investment decision.

This Memorandum contains forward looking statements and information that is based on our beliefs as well as assumptions made by and information currently available to us. When used in this Memorandum, words such as "anticipate," "believes," "estimate," "expect," and, depending on the context, "will," "intends" and similar expressions, are intended to identify forward looking statements. Such statements reflect our current assumptions with respect to future events and are subject to certain risks, uncertainties and further assumptions, including the specific risk factors described herein. If one or more of these risks or uncertainties materialize, or if underlying assumptions prove incorrect, our actual results may vary materially from those anticipated, believed, estimated or expected.

1. New Venture

Our management team of Meredith Schanderfrug and Jose Montes-Rios has experience in awesome enterprises. However, we are a new company and are advancing into a new venture in a very competitive field. Our success will depend in part on our ability to deal with the problems, expenses and delays frequently associated with establishing a new business venture and obtaining sufficient market penetration and acceptance of our services. General economic conditions may affect our activities. Interest rates, general levels of employment, economic activity, and other general economic factors may affect the value of an investment in us. It is impossible to predict with any certainty the economic outlook or future of our business or the national economy as a whole.

2. Limited Operating History

We were formed on _____ ___, 20__. While our business plan was in development prior to formation, our active operations are not expected to begin until the fourth quarter of _____. Accordingly, our operating history is minimal, and it will be difficult for you to evaluate our business and future prospects. In your evaluation, you must consider the risks, expenses and difficulties that we will face and that are frequently encountered by new companies, particularly companies in competitive markets. To address these risks we must, among other things, raise enough money to fully fund our operations, effectively manage costs and quickly build a client base. We can make no assurances that we will be successful in addressing these risks, and the failure to meet these challenges could have a material adverse effect on us.

3. Dependence Upon Offering

Because we are a developing company, we have not immediate sources of revenue and have only a limited amount of working capital. We are intending to use the monies raised under the Offering as working capital to and to begin operating our business. However, we can make no assurance that all or enough of the Units will be sold or that our future revenues will meet our projections. We will not escrow any subscription funds and we use and spend investment funds received as the money comes in. [Check with your advisors on this strategy. Some investors want their money held in escrow and only released to the company when the full amount is raised.] Therefore, if our business fails you will lose your entire investments. Even if all of the Units are sold we may still have insufficient capital to fund our business and may still need to pursue other financing alternatives.

4. Reliance Upon Officers, Managers and Key Personnel

We are, at present, completely dependent upon the personal efforts and abilities of our principals, Meredith Schanderfrug and Jose Montes-Rios. If either Meredith or Jose become unable to run our operation, or if we cannot assemble the core team of business talent, we will face a significant risk that our business will be unable to function properly and will fail.

5. Conflicts of Interest

Because some of our officers and managers may initially work in other capacities, it is possible that conflicts of interest may arise. Such potential conflicts of interest may have a negative effect on the company's performance.

6. Lack of Business

Our success will depend on our ability to generate awesome distribution and sales. If we are unable to capture a portion of the awesome market it will be difficult to operate our business effectively. Alternatively, even if we are successful in capturing a market share, if the overall economy falls we may still have a hard time generating sufficient revenues for our business to succeed.

7. Competition

Awesome Co., LLC will be competing against established awesome companies in this region. Some companies will have significantly more capital than we will have. We cannot guarantee that we will be able to successfully compete with the existing awesome firms in the marketplace.

8. Management of Continued Growth

If we are successful we will need to expand our operations. To do this, we will need to effectively plan and manage our future growth. Depending on how fast we grow, it could strain our management, operational and financial resources. We must ensure that proper planning is in place to manage any expansion without compromising our existing business.

9. Value of Our Interests

The purchase price for the Units was arbitrarily set by our Managers. Because our Interests are not publicly traded, we cannot tell what the future value of the Interests will be. The value of our Interests will continue to be subject to our discretionary determination in accordance with what we expect to be a reasonable value. In the unlikely event we become a public reporting company, and our Interests are placed for public transactions on any exchange, market or over-the-counter trading system, fair market valuation will play a principal role in future pricing information.

10. Non-Registered Securities; No Public Market; Liquidity

We are a private company and are not trading on any exchange or bulletin board. There is no public market for the Units and underlying Interests and we do not know if such a market will develop. Neither the Units nor the underlying Interests have been registered under the Securities Act or under any state securities law in reliance upon certain exemptions provided in such laws. The Units and underlying Interests cannot be resold in any state unless they are subsequently registered or unless an exemption from registration is available. There is no definite plan to register the Units or underlying Interests in the future and you will have no right to require us to make such a registration. Consequently, you may not be able to liquidate your investment in us and may be required to hold your Interests for an indefinite period of time. Accordingly, investing in our stock is not suitable if you need investment liquidity.

11. Projections

Because we are newly formed with no revenue we have not prepared audited financial statements. As well, we have not prepared financial projections for this Memorandum. While management believes its internal projections may be met, we make no guarantees at all with respect to the accuracy and forecasting ability of our projections.

12. Majority Ownership Held by Management

Assuming that all of the Units are sold our principals, Meredith Schanderfrug and Jose Montes-Rios, will beneficially own fifty-six and one half percent (56.5%) of our issued and outstanding Interests. In the event the eight percent (8%) of Interests held in reserve are sold Meredith Schanderfrug and Jose Montes-Rios will beneficially own fifty-two percent (52%) of our issued and outstanding Interests. Accordingly, Meredith Schanderfrug and Jose Montes-Rios will continue to be able to control the outcome of all matters submitted to a vote of our members, including the election of managers, amendments to our Articles of Organization and approval of significant transactions, such as a merger, or a sale of all or substantially all of our assets. This voting control could also effectively delay or prevent a change in control that might be beneficial to other shareholders.

13. Dilution

At present, our primary financing mechanism is the sale of equity capital. Because we already have a significant number of Interests outstanding, immediately after you purchase Units the value of your underlying Interests will be decreased due to dilution factors. In addition, any other sales of our Interests that we make in the future will dilute your investment again. Finally, our officers, managers and consultants may receive stock or other equity grants in connection with their services, and these grants would further dilute your investment.

14. Phantom Income

Because we are a limited liability company, our net profits and losses flow through to our shareholders, and the taxes are paid by our shareholders at their personal income tax rates. However, there may be circumstances where we are unable to distribute any or all of our net profits to our shareholders, as we need the funds to grow our business. However, regardless of whether or not we distribute all or any of our net profits to our shareholders, the Internal Revenue Service will calculate all taxes payable on the basis that shareholders have in fact received all net profits that they were entitled to. If we are unable to distribute all or any of our net profits to our shareholders, you could be assessed for and be required to pay taxes on monies that you do not, in fact, receive. We can make no guarantees that we will always be able to distribute all or sufficient net profits to you to offset any taxes that you are required to pay.

INVESTOR SUITABILITY STANDARDS

15. General Offering Investment Characteristics; Transferability of Interests

Investment in the Units and underlying Interests offered hereby involves significant risks. See "Risk Factors". Neither the Units nor the underlying Interests offered herein have been nor will they be registered under the Securities Act. We have no obligation or intention to register any class of our securities for resale under any federal or state securities law. Further, no resale or transfer will be permitted except in accordance with the provisions of the Securities Act, the rules and regulations thereunder, and any applicable state securities laws. This is a private offering made only by delivery of a copy of this Memorandum to you. You will be required to represent to us that you are familiar with and understand the terms of the Offering and that you are acquiring the Units for your own account as an investment, and not with any intention of reselling or redistributing your Interests, either in whole or in part.

16. Investor Suitability Standards

An investment in us is suitable only for those investors who have adequate financial means and no need for liquidity with respect to their investment. The Offering will be sold to investors who are "accredited" within the meaning of Regulation D of the Securities Act, investors who receive assistance from a qualified Purchaser Representative, and to a limited number of non-accredited investors. You will be required to represent in writing in the Subscription Agreement and Purchaser Suitability Questionnaire that you meet our suitability standards. Also, be aware that certain states may impose different or additional suitability standards that may be more restrictive than those set out below and even if you are eligible under our standards, you may be barred from subscribing under the laws of your home state.

An "*Accredited Investor*" is defined in Regulation D to include: (i) a natural person whose individual net worth (excluding home, home furnishings and automobiles), or joint net worth with such person's spouse, exceeds $1 million at the time of purchase; or (ii) a natural person who has an individual income in excess of $200,000 in each of the two most recent years or joint income with that person's spouse in excess of $300,000 in each of those years and who reasonably expects to reach the same income level in the current year; or (iii) a business entity, not formed for the specific purpose of acquiring the Interests offered, with total assets in excess of $5,000,000; or (iv) an entity in which all of the equity owners are Accredited Investors.

A *"Purchaser Representative-Assisted Investor"* is an investor who does not meet the income and asset test for Accredited Investor, but receives advice from a Purchaser Representative prior to subscribing and confirms in writing, the name of their Purchaser Representative at the time of subscription.

A Purchaser Representative is an individual who:

Is not connected to us by way of being an officer, director, employee, affiliate or member owing 10% or more of our Interests;

Has such knowledge and experience in financial and business matters that they are capable of evaluating, alone, or together with other purchaser representatives of the purchaser, or together with the purchaser, the merits and risks of the prospective investment; and

Advises the purchaser, in writing, before the purchaser enters into a subscription agreement, of any past (two years only), present or future material relationship they have had with us and whether they have ever received any money or other compensation for such material relationship.

A *"Non-Accredited Investor"* is an investor who does not meet the income and asset test set out above and does not have a Purchaser Representative. While there is no regulated minimum income and asset test for a Non-Accredited investor, we have determined that we will not sell Units to any investors unless they meet the following criteria:

(i)the Non-Accredited Investor expects to have during the current and next three years, taxable income of $60,000, or more; or

(ii)the Non-Accredited Investor is a family member or individual with a substantial pre-existing business, or has a personal relationship with one of our directors or officers.

Please note that Nevada law prohibits us from allowing more than twenty-five (25) non-accredited investors to invest under the Offering. We may sell Units to an unlimited number of accredited or Purchaser Representative-Assisted investors.

USE OF PROCEEDS

To date, minimal funds have been raised on our behalf. We have been funded through the personal efforts of Meredith Schanderfrug and Jose Montes-Rios, who have received common interests in consideration for their cash and note contributions of $10,000.

We must raise a minimum of $800,000 in order to commence operations and proceed with our business plan.

		Amount
(a)	Purchase of Equipment	$450,000
(b)	Costs of the Offering (includes legal, accounting, printing and regulatory filing costs)	25,000
(c)	Working Capital	325,000
	Total	**$800,000**

We have not included any amount for commission as the Offering will be sold only by our officers, managers and principals, none of whom will receive any commission in connection with their efforts.

We will spend the funds raised through the Offering to purchase the equipment and begin our business operations set out in "Description of the Business." There may be circumstances where, for sound business reasons, we need to reallocate funds within the categories set out above. We have the sole authority to change the allocation of funds if necessary.

Should we sell all of the Units we should have sufficient working capital available to fund our business operation for a twelve month period following the Offering.

17. Audited Financial Statements

Because we are a new entity with no operating history, we have not prepared audited financial statements. [Be sure to talk to your own attorney about this issue.]

DESCRIPTION OF THE COMPANY

18. General

We were formed in Nevada on _____ _____, 20__, as Awesome Company, LLC, a Nevada Limited Liability Company. We were formed specifically to operate an awesome company.

19. Management

We currently have Meredith Schanderfrug and Jose Montes-Rios serving as its managers and officers. See "Management of the Company."

20. Insurance

We will maintain insurance coverage, including general liability, fire and extended coverage. We believe that this coverage will be adequate to protect our business, assets and operations. We may also explore the possibility of obtaining managers and officers insurance in the future.

21. Financial Statements

We intend to provide our interest holders with financial statements annually, at their request. At this time we have no intention of preparing audited financial statements, however, if and when we do make such a change, we will offer to provide the audited financial statements to our members.

22. Description of Property

We are looking to lease approximately 2,000 square feet of space for our business office in_____, _____. The company has not yet identified a property.

23. Employees and Contract Labor

During our preliminary start-up stage, we have had no full-time employees. We have relied on our principals, Meredith Schanderfrug and Jose Montes-Rios, to provide all required services.

Over the six months following the Offering, and subject to achieving our goals (see "Business of the Company"), we anticipate that the following employees and contract labor personnel will be required:

[List employee needs]

We anticipate that additional support employees will be added as the need dictates. We have budgeted approximately $_____ per month for salaries and employment expenses during our first year of active operations, which are expected to be paid from revenues.

24. Legal Proceedings

To the best of our knowledge we are not a party to or aware of an existing, pending or contemplated legal proceedings, nor are any of our managers, officers or key management personnel.

BUSINESS OF THE COMPANY

25. Executive Summary

We will be an awesome company as follows:

26. Mission Statement

The mission of Awesome Company can be expressed succinctly: To make money, and be awesome doing so.

This simply expressed mission does have multiple implications, which are as follows:

27. Company Summary

Awesome Company is a start-up enterprise that will:

28. Products

The company will initially produce and market:

29. Product Description

We can describe our awesome products as:

30. Competitive Comparison

We have two levels of competition within the awesome industry. They are:

31. Technology

We will take advantage of the latest awesome technologies to:

32. Future Products

We will help promote and maintain interest in our awesome products by:

33. SWOT Analysis

In our strength, weakness, opportunity and threat analysis we see the following:

Strengths

• We believe ourselves to be awesome.

Weaknesses

• No one knows we are awesome.

Opportunities

• Significant opportunity exists when customers learn we are awesome.

Threats

• Other awesome companies, with more awesome bank accounts, do exist in the market.

34. Market Analysis Summary

The awesome market began to establish itself in the 1980's, experienced rapid growth in the early 1990's, and is now settling into a mature phase of slow, but steady, annual growth. Most of this growth is:

Market Segmentation

The awesome market is divided into two broad types of accounts: _____ and _____.

Target Market Segment Strategy

Defining our market segments in this fashion provides us with an outline for allocating our marketing resources.

Industry Analysis

Industry analysis information is presented in the following subtopics.

Competition and Buying Patterns

Awesome consumers are an inherently adventuresome lot who enjoy _____.

Main Competitors

There are two primary competitors in the domestic awesome sector of our market:

Strategy and Implementation Summary
As we are a new company, our strategy will progress through several stages:

Value Proposition
Our value proposition is offering our customers awesomeness as follows:

Marketing Strategy
Our Marketing Strategy is comprised of many awesome elements:

Product Packaging
Our awesomeness will be packaged in awesome ways:

Service Provision
It is essential that we build strong relationships with our distributors and accounts, and to do this we need to provide excellent service and:

Pricing Strategy
Our product pricing will be at or slightly less than that of our competitors, as follows:

Promotion Strategy
Our promotional strategy will be designed to enhance the visibility of our company and our products, as follows:

Advertising
We will be very selective about the types of paid advertising that we utilize. Our strategy will be to:

Internet Marketing
Many people now use the internet as their first option for obtaining information about a subject or business. With this being the case, we will:

Public Relations
There are a variety of ways that we can obtain positive publicity to build our image and reputation. We will:

Distribution Strategy
We will use a distribution strategy of:
Sales Strategy
Our sales strategy will be:

Sales Forecast
Our sales forecast is charted as follows:

Corporate Social Responsibility
Awesome Company intends to participate in a wide range of social responsible programs to invest back into the community. These include:

Production Summary
Our production system shall be designed to operate with high efficiency and yield the best possible product. This shall be accomplished by:

Suppliers and Raw Materials
In recent years the variety and availability of awesome raw materials has increased dramatically. This will allow us to:

Human Resources Summary
At Awesome Company, we recognize that while personnel are important at every company, they are especially crucial to a small, growing company. All of our employees will need to be flexible and multi-functional. Each one will also serve as an ambassador of our company when they deal with the public, our suppliers, or our customers. As we grow as a company, our employees will take on new duties and responsibilities. Thus, it is essential that we hire and retain excellent personnel, and motivate them to perform to the best of their abilities.

To get the best possible performance from our employees, we will emphasize the following strategies:

Management Team
The management team is comprised of Meredith Schanderfrug and Jose Montes-Rios with the assistance of well qualified stakeholders.

Meredith Schanderfrug has both advanced technical training and extensive experience in the awesome industry. Her education and experience includes:

Jose Montes-Rios has the following relevant training and experience:

Personnel Plan

Initially, we will have very few employees, as Meredith Schanderfrug and Jose Montes-Rios will be performing the majority of production and sales work, and will manage the company on a day-to-day basis.

Financial Plan

Our full, detailed financial projections are available as follows:

MANAGEMENT OF THE COMPANY

Directors, Officers and Key Management

Our managers, officers and key management personnel are as follows:

Officer and Director Salaries and other Benefits

None of our directors, officers or key personnel has received any cash payments for services they have provided to date. Meredith Schanderfrug and Jose Montes-Rios have invested a total of $10,000 in cash and promissory notes. They have also contributed intellectual property related to the awesomeness product. Together they have received 520,000 Interests in consideration of their investment. This represents a 52% ownership interest, once the first round of 16 units and the second round, if any, of 8 units are sold.

Meredith Schanderfrug and Jose Montes-Rios are each donating their time to get our business established and will continue to donate their time as needed. As majority owners, they will receive a pro-rata share of our net profits.

27. Option Plan

We do not have a stock option plan in place for our managers, officers, consultants or employees. At this time we do not intend to implement such a plan. If we change our plans in the future, any stock option plan implemented would have to be approved by our shareholders prior to becoming effective.

RELATED PARTY TRANSACTIONS

None of our directors, officers or senior management receives any material benefits, directly or indirectly, through their involvement with other organizations doing business with us. Our directors and officers will use their best efforts to ensure that no such conflicts arise and will act at all times in our best interests.

28. Security Ownership of Directors, Officers and Senior Management

Meredith Schanderfrug and Jose Montes-Rios, our principals, managers and officers, hold a total of 520,000 Interests. This represents 100% of our issued and outstanding Interests prior to the Offering, and will represent 56.5% of our issued and outstanding Interests after the Offering, if we sell all 16 Units.

29. Indemnification of Directors and Officers

Our operating agreement provides for the indemnification of our officers and managers, for non-derivative actions. Indemnification covers litigation expenses, judgments, fines and settlement payments. In derivative actions, indemnification does not cover judgments or settlements paid, and expenses of an unsuccessful defense are covered only if the court approves; indemnification in derivative actions is permitted otherwise. There are certain preconditions to the right of an officer or director to receive indemnification, including requirements that the person must have acted with due care, in good faith and in the reasonable belief that their acts were in our best interests. If the officer or director is successful on the merits in a proceeding or on any claim, issue or matter therein, related expenses are covered without the need to satisfy the stated preconditions.

It is the opinion of the Securities and Exchange Commission that indemnifying our officers and managers is against public policy, and therefore it does not consider our indemnification provisions to be enforceable. Accordingly, if any liabilities arise under the Securities Act, our officers and directors may be found liable for such liabilities by the Securities and Exchange Commission, even if they may be indemnified under our bylaws.

30. Principal Shareholders (including Beneficial Shareholders)

Before beginning the Offering we have two members classified as "beneficial" Interest holders. A beneficial Interest holders is defined as an individual, entity or group of affiliated persons who own 5% or more of our issued interests. After the Offering we will have a total of 2 beneficial Interests, assuming that pre-Offering commitments to purchase Units are met, as follows:

Beneficial Shareholder Name and Address	Number of interests held	Number of Options Granted	Ownership Percentage Prior To the Offering	Ownership Percentage following the Offering
Meredith Schanderfrug *Founder, Manager, and Officer* address:_____	260,000	None	50%	28.25%
Jose Montes-Rios *Founder, Manager and Officer* address:_____	260,000	None	50%	28.25%

PLAN OF DISTRIBUTION

31. Authorized Interests

We were formed as a limited liability company with no set number of authorized Interests. We are basing our ownership percentages on the issuance of 1,000,000 Interests. A total of 520,000 Interests have been issued to date.

32. Rights, Preferences, Privileges and Restrictions on Securities

Members holding Interests of our company are entitled to one vote per Interest at all meetings of the members. Members also have the right to receive distributions if, as and when we declare any, and to participate on a pro rata basis in any distribution of our property or assets on to our liquidation, winding up or other dissolution.

None of our Interests have any pre-emptive or conversion rights. Provisions as to modification, amendment or variation of such rights or such provisions are contained in Chapter 86 of the Nevada Revised Statutes.

33. Distributions

To date, we have not paid any cash distributions on our Interests. If we are successful, we intend to make distributions in the future. The amount of any such distributions will be dependent on our total revenues and any amounts we need to retain to finance the growth and development of our business. All decisions on whether or not we pay cash distributions will be made in our sole discretion.

34. Interests Being Offered

We are offering a total of 16 Units, each containing 25,000 common interests, or 400,000 common interests for sale under this Memorandum. The price per Unit is $50,000, or $2.00 per membership interest. We require you to purchase a minimum of one Unit, or $50,000 under the Offering. However, we do reserve the right, in our sole discretion, to accept investments for less than one Unit.

35. Regulation D, Rule 506

The Units and underlying Interests being offered are being sold as unregistered securities, pursuant to an exemption found in Regulation D, Rule 506. Regulation D, Rule 506 provides that a company may sell unregistered securities under this provision to accredited investors, purchaser representative-assisted investors and non-accredited investors. However, we are limited to selling Units to a maximum of 35 non-accredited investors (of which only 25 may be Nevada residents). See "Investor Suitability Standards" for a detailed definition of accredited, purchaser representative-assisted and non-accredited investors.

36. Resale Restrictions

The Units and underlying Interests are subject to both the Resale Restrictions set out in Rule 144 of the Securities Act as well as those contained in Rule 502(d) of Regulation D to the Securities Act.

Rule 144 requires that all securities being sold as unregistered, or "restricted" securities (i.e., securities not sold under a Registration Statement or Prospectus), be subject to a one-year hold period, commencing on the date that the securities are issued. During this one-year hold period, the securities purchased may not be transferred or re-sold.

Rule 144 further imposes a limitation on the number of Interests that may be sold in each instance following the expiration of the one-year hold period and other pre-conditions to such sales. You must consult your own securities advisor prior to making any attempt to resell Units you acquire under the Offering.

Rule 502(d) of Regulation D provides that securities acquired through a transaction under Regulation D may not be resold without first being registered under the Securities Act, unless an exemption from registration is available. Rule 502(d) further requires us to ensure that all Share Certificates representing Interests sold under the Offering have the following legend printed on them:

THE SECURITIES OFFERED HEREBY HAVE NOT BEEN REGISTERED UNDER THE SECURITIES ACT OF 1933, AS AMENDED (THE "SECURITIES ACT"), OR ANY STATE SECURITIES LAWS. THE SECURITIES REPRESENTED BY THIS CERTIFICATE HAVE BEEN ACQUIRED FOR INVESTMENT, AND NOT WITH A VIEW TO, OR IN CONNECTION WITH, THE SALE OR DISPOSITION THEREOF. NO SUCH SALE OR DISPOSITION MAY BE MADE WITHOUT (1) AN EFFECTIVE REGISTRATION STATEMENT RELATING THERETO, OR AN OPINION OF COUNSEL (SATISFACTORY TO THE COMPANY) THAT SUCH REGISTRATION IS NOT REQUIRED UNDER THE SECURITIES ACT; AND (2) IN COMPLIANCE WITH ANY APPLICABLE STATE SECURITIES LAWS.

37. Prior Sales of Securities

Prior to the Offering, we issued a total of 520,000 interests to Meredith Schanderfrug and Jose Montes-Rios, representing a 52% interest in us, assuming all Units are sold in the first two rounds of funding.

38. Fully Diluted Share Capital

Upon the successful completion of this Offering, and assuming that all Units are sold, we will have a total of 920,000 membership Interests of common stock issued and outstanding.

There are no other rights to purchase any form of security interest in us outstanding.

39. Plan of Capitalization

Should we sell all 16 Units offered, we will receive net proceeds of approximately $800,000. We will use all investment funds received to begin our business operations. We will also use some of the net proceeds for working capital and administrative costs until our business becomes profitable. See "Use of Proceeds."

MANAGEMENT'S DISCUSSION AND ANALYSIS OF FINANCIAL CONDITION AND RESULTS OF OPERATIONS

In this Memorandum we have made certain statements of a forward-looking nature relating to future events or our future financial performance. As a prospective investor, you are cautioned that these statements are only predictions. These statements involve risks and uncertainties and actual events or results may differ materially. We have prepared all forward-looking statements internally, and they have not been reviewed by our accountants. Accordingly, all forward-looking financial information provided in this Memorandum may be incorrect. In evaluating such statements, you should specifically consider the various factors identified in this Memorandum, including the matters set forth under the heading "Risk Factors," which could cause our actual results to differ materially from our forward-looking statements.

40. Operations to Date

We are a development stage company with no operations to date. We expect to begin active operations in the fourth quarter of_____, as soon as we have completed this Offering.

FINANCIAL INFORMATION

41. Financial Statements

We were incorporated on _____ _____, 20___, and have not yet commenced active business operations. We have not prepared audited financial statements as there are no funds to audit.

AVAILABLE INFORMATION

You and your investment advisors are welcome to communicate with Meredith Schanderfrug at 555-555-7799.

Meredith Schanderfrug and Jose Montes-Rios will answer inquiries from you and your investment advisors concerning our business, our management or any other matter relating to an investment in us. Meredith Schanderfrug and Jose Montes-Rios will also give you and your representatives the opportunity to obtain any additional information (to the extent we possess such information or can acquire it without unreasonable effort or expense) necessary to verify the accuracy of any statements or information contained in this Memorandum.

- END -

EXHIBIT "A"

SUBSCRIPTION AGREEMENT

To be completed by all Subscribers

I, the undersigned, subject to the terms and conditions hereof and the provisions of the Awesome Company, LLC., Private Placement Memorandum dated _____ _____ 20___, hereby tender this Subscription Agreement, together with a certified or cashier's check, payable to **Awesome Company, LLC**, for an aggregate of:

> _____ **Units, at a price of $50,000 per Unit, for a total amount payable of $_____.**
>
> **(each Unit consists of 25,000 Interests)**
>
> **NAME(S) IN WHICH YOU WANT YOUR INTERESTS ISSUED:**
>
> _____

I confirm that upon Awesome Company accepting my subscription, this Subscription Agreement to purchase Units will be considered final and irrevocable, subject only to the limitations set out below.

1. **Termination of Offering**. The Offering of the Units shall terminate upon the earlier of:

a. The date all Units are subscribed for; or

b. _____ 20___, unless prior to such date, the Company notifies subscribers in writing that the Offering has been extended to a date specified in such notice, which date shall not be later than _____ 20___; or

c. The date the Company, in its sole discretion, notifies subscribers in writing that the Offering is terminated. It is agreed that the Company may terminate the Offering at any time for any reason.

2. **Receipt of Private Placement Memorandum**. I acknowledge that I have received and read a copy of the Private Placement Memorandum relating to the sale of Units by the Company and I am aware of the

significant economic and other risks involved in purchasing the Units as described in the Private Placement Memorandum dated _____ 20___.

3. **Acquisition**. I acknowledge, agree, represent and warrant to the Company and its officers, managers and Interest holders that:

a. All statements set forth in the Purchaser Suitability Questionnaire accompanying my Subscription Agreement are true and correct and may be relied upon by the Company.

b. (i) the Units are being offered and sold in reliance upon the exemption from registration provided by Section 4(2) and Regulation D, Rule 506 of the Securities Act of 1933, as amended (the "Securities Act") for the private offering of securities; (ii) there are substantial restrictions on the transferability of the Units and the underlying Interests, (iii) there is no public market for the Units and the underlying Interests, and I will be required to bear the economic risk of my investment for an indefinite length of time, (iv) I may not be able to liquidate this investment in the event of any financial emergency, and (v) the Company is not contractually obligated to register the Units or the underlying Interests under the Securities Act and these securities may not be sold or otherwise transferred without registration under the Securities Act, unless an exemption from registration is available.

c. I have received all information that I consider necessary or desirable to my making an informed investment decision about the Company.

d. I have had an opportunity to ask questions of and receive satisfactory answers from Company-authorized representatives concerning the terms and conditions of the Offering and the Company in general. I have been given the opportunity to review any documents and any other information I have requested from the Company to verify information provided to me and to answer any questions I have concerning the Company's business affairs and financial condition.

e. No federal or state agencies have passed upon, or made any finding or determination as to the fairness of the Offering, and no federal or state agency has recommended or endorsed the purchase of Units.

f. I am at least 21 years of age. I have adequate means of providing for my current and future financial needs (and possible personal contingencies) and I have no need now, and anticipate no need in the foreseeable future, to sell any of the Units or the underlying Interests.

g. All of the information, representations and warranties made by me in my Subscription Agreement and Purchaser Suitability Questionnaire, or that I may have otherwise given or made to the Company are correct and complete as of the date hereof, and may be relied upon by the Company. If there are any material changes to the information I have provided to the Company I will immediately furnish such revised or corrected information to the Company in writing.

h. I have enough knowledge and experience in financial and business matters to make me capable of evaluating the merits and risks of investment in the Units or the underlying Interests and to make an informed decision.

i. I am acquiring the Units for my own account and not for anyone else, nor am I purchasing the Units with the intent of reselling the Units or the underlying Interests at a later date.

j. The following statements regarding this transaction applies:

THE SECURITIES OFFERED HEREBY HAVE NOT BEEN REGISTERED UNDER THE SECURITIES ACT OF 1933, AS AMENDED (THE "SECURITIES ACT"), OR ANY STATE SECURITIES LAWS. THE SECURITIES REPRESENTED BY THIS CERTIFICATE HAVE BEEN ACQUIRED FOR INVESTMENT, AND NOT WITH A VIEW TO, OR IN CONNECTION WITH, THE SALE OR DISPOSITION THEREOF. NO SUCH SALE OR DISPOSITION MAY BE MADE WITHOUT (1) AN EFFECTIVE REGISTRATION STATEMENT RELATING THERETO, OR AN OPINION OF COUNSEL (SATISFACTORY TO THE COMPANY) THAT SUCH REGISTRATION IS NOT REQUIRED UNDER THE SECURITIES ACT; AND (2) IN COMPLIANCE WITH ANY APPLICABLE STATE SECURITIES LAWS.

Type of Vesting (Check One)

(a)   Individual Ownership (one signature required)

(b)   Joint tenants with right of survivorship (both or all parties' signatures required)

(c)   Community Property (one signature required if Interests held in one name; two if Interests held in both names)

(d)   Tenants in Common (both or all parties' signatures required)

(e)   Other: _____

Dated this _____ day of _____, 20___.

_____
Signature of Investor(s)

_____
Signature of Joint Investor (if applicable)

_____
Address

ACCEPTED AS OF: _____, 20___
Awesome Company, LLC
a Nevada Limited Liability Company

_____
Authorized Signatory

EXHIBIT "B"
PURCHASER SUITABIILTY
QUESTIONNAIRE

To be completed by all Subscribers

[This is the self-certifying form]

This Offering is open to Accredited, Purchaser Representative-Assisted and Non-Accredited Investors. Regulation D, Rule 506 of the Securities Act requires us to take steps to determine investor status prior to sales of securities. This acknowledgment must be answered fully and returned to us along with your subscription agreement, so that we may ensure we comply with the Securities Act. All information will be held in the strictest confidence and used only to determine investor status. No information will be disclosed other than as required by law or regulation, other demand by proper legal process or in litigation involving us or our affiliates, controlling persons, officers, directors, partners, employees, shareholders, attorneys or agents.

1. <u>Personal Data</u>

   Name _____

   Address of principal residence _____

   (include city, state and zip) _____

   Telephone number (____) _____

2. Manner of Solicitation:

   How did you learn of our investment opportunity? (i.e., by personal contact or acquaintance with an investment advisor or counselor, with on of our officers or directors, a broker-dealer or otherwise, naming such person):

personal contact with an officer or director   through a broker-dealer or financial advisor

_____ (name of person)

other: _____ (please describe)

3. <u>Net Worth and Income</u> (Please answer all questions)

<u>Accredited Investors:</u>

My individual net worth or joint net worth (exclusive of home, home furnishings and automobiles) with my spouse exceeds $1,000,000. (_____Yes _____No).

I had an individual income in excess of $200,000 in each of the two most recent years or joint income with my spouse in excess of $300,000 in each of these years and reasonably expect reaching the same income level in the current year. (_____Yes _____No).

<u>Purchaser Representative:</u>

I have a Purchaser Representative (as defined in Rule 501(H) of Regulation D of the Securities Act) who assisted me in connection with evaluating the merits and risks of my investment in the Interests. (_____Yes _____No).

If "Yes", the name, company affiliation (if any), business address and business telephone number of my Purchaser Representative is:

_____

_____

My overall commitment to investments that are not readily marketable is not disproportionate to my net worth, and my investment in the Interests will not cause my overall commitments to become disproportionate (_____Yes _____No).

I have adequate means of providing for my current needs and personal and family contingencies, I have no need for liquidity in my investment in the Interests, and I am able to bear the economic risks of investment (_____Yes _____No).

<u>Non-Accredited Investors:</u>

I have a net worth of the Units subscribed for in excess of five times the purchase price of the Units subscribed for, and expect to have during the current and next three years taxable income of $60,000, or more and have a net worth (exclusive of home, home furnishings and automobiles) of $60,000 in excess of the purchase price (_____Yes _____No).

My overall commitment to investments which are not readily marketable is not disproportionate to my net worth, and my investment in the Units will not cause my overall commitments to become disproportionate (_____Yes _____No).

I have adequate means of providing for my current needs and personal and family contingencies, I have no need for liquidity in my investment in the Units, and I am able to bear the economic risks of investment (_____Yes _____No).

4. Reference:

Please provide the name of your accountant, attorney or other individual familiar with your finances who may be contacted to verify financial information contained in this questionnaire:

Name _____

Address _____

Relationship _____

Telephone number(_____) _____

5. Representations:

I represent: That I have // have not received the Private Placement Memorandum ("PPM") dated _____, 20___; that I have sufficient knowledge and experience in similar programs or investments to evaluate the merits and risks of an investment in the company because of my background, employment experience, family or financial situation or economic bargaining power; that I agree to fulfill the education requirement detailed in the PPM; that I agree to forfeit my interests if I do not meet the education requirement; that I have received and have had access to material and relevant information enabling me to make an informed investment and/or exchange decision; that all information I have requested has been furnished to me; that I am able to bear the economic risk of loss of the entire investment that I may make in Awesome Company, LLC; and that the information provided herein is complete, true, correct and may be relied upon.

6. NASD Affiliation:

Do you have any direct or indirect affiliation or association with any person or firm that is a member of the National Association of Securities Dealers, Inc., as an officer, director, shareholder, partner, principal, registered representative, employee or otherwise? (_____Yes _____No). If yes, provide details.

INVESTOR

Date:_____

_____

Signature of Investor

_____

Type or Print Name

_____

Social Security Number

JOINT INVESTOR (IF APPLICABLE)

Date:_____

_____

Signature of Investor

_____

Type or Print Name

_____

Social Security Number

Appendix C
Real Estate Risk Factors

General Real Estate Risks

Our Company will be subject to the risks of purchasing, developing, financing and selling real estate. More specifically, our Company will be subject to all risks incident to ownership and financing of real estate and interests therein, many of which relate to the general illiquidity of real estate investments. These risks include, but are not limited to, changes in general or local economic conditions, changes in interest rates and the availability of financing which may render the purchase, sale or refinancing of a property difficult or unattractive and which may make debt service burdensome, floods, earthquakes, storms, hurricanes and other acts of God, acts of terrorists, changes in real estate and zoning laws increases in real estate taxes , federal or local economic or rent controls, and other factors beyond the control of the Company. The illiquidity of real estate investments may also impair the ability of our Company to respond promptly to changing circumstances.

Our Company can provide no assurance that any investment will be successful. Problems and delays may be encountered, including increased capital costs, construction and materials costs, poor or improper architectural design or plans, defaults by contractors, delayed development schedules, defect caused by and poor workmanship by contractors, litigation and/or liens involving contractors and/or subcontractors, improper or poor quality materials used in construction and otherwise. Some of the other elements of risk (as discussed herein) may also impact our Company's schedules for acquiring, developing and selling properties.

Damage and Insurance Issues.

If our Company suffers losses that are not covered by insurance or that are in excess of insurance coverage limits, our Company could lose anticipated profits and investment capital. Property owned by our Company could be adversely affected by the occurrence of floods, land subsidence, soil conditions, mold, earthquakes, other acts of God, acts by terrorists, and other factors beyond the control of our Company. Damage caused by any of these events might not be covered by insurance.

Our Company will maintain, or cause to be maintained, comprehensive insurance on each of our Company's properties. Insurance coverages on a property will include liability and fire insurance and extended coverage insurance in the amounts sufficient to permit the replacement of the property in the event of a total loss, subject to applicable deductibles. However, there are certain types of losses, generally of a catastrophic nature, such as floods, hurricanes, earthquakes, and acts of terrorism—along with certain environmental losses, such as those connected with asbestos, mold, radon or hazardous wastes—that may be uninsurable or not insurable at a price our Company can afford. Inflation, changes in building codes and ordinances, environmental considerations and other factors also might make it impracticable to use insurance proceeds to replace a property after it has been damaged or destroyed. Under such circumstances, the insurance proceeds our Company receives might not be adequate to restore its economic position with respect to the affected property. If any of these or similar events occur, it may reduce the return from a property and the value of the investment.

Environmental Liabilities

As with most real estate, our Company faces risks of unanticipated environmental liabilities. Our Company could become liable for the costs of removing environmental hazards even after buying the properties without knowledge of the problems. In addition, our Company's investigations of potential environmental liabilities could be incomplete, thereby giving rise to additional unanticipated remediation costs. Any such costs could adversely and materially affect the success of the investment in the related property. Insurance may not be available to reduce the negative effect of these remediation costs.

Economic Downturn/Oversupply

There is no guarantee as to what will happen with the national economy or the economy of the area(s) in which our business will be conducted. Either or both of those economies may take a turn for the worse, or interest rates on real estate loans may increase. In any case, there is no guarantee that properties will be sold within the time anticipated by our Company. All of these occurrences could have a materially adverse financial effect on our Company and on the investors.

Cost Overruns

It is possible that the costs of developing and marketing the property will be significantly higher than our Company expects. This could have a materially adverse financial effect on our Company and on the returns to the investors.

Appendix D
Funding Comparison

Type	Cost	Payback Terms	Sizes	For	Against
Personal Savings	Lost interest	None		Easy, cheap	Risk of loss
Friends & Family	Usually good rate or none	Very flexible		Flexible, best value	Can create friction
Home Mortgages-Traditional or Seconds	5-8% or 7-14% on equity loans	Very long and flexible	80-100% + of home equity value	Cheapest, longest term	Your house is at risk in the event of non-payment
Credit cards	16-23%	40 – 60 months	$3,000-10,000	Easy, qualifying, no collateral	Small amounts
Person-to-person on-line networks such as lendingclub or prosper.com	6% - up	Varies	Up to $50,000	Quick response, fast-growing resource	
Suppliers	Free	30 days +/-		Inexpensive, unsecured	short term
Commercial mortgage	7-9%	25 year payment; all due in 10 years	$300,000 +; 75% of appraisal		
Specialized lenders (industry expertise, auto, business brokers, high tech, specialized equipment,	12-18%	5-7 years	Varies	Accessible through dealer, who is motivated to make sale of equipment or business; payback terms more	Debt service can be high

computers, phones, etc.				favorable than bank	
Leasing companies	12-18%	5-7 years	Varies	Same as above; also 100% financing	
SBA loan guarantee programs	7-9%	7-20 years	$50,000-$1,000,000	Longest payback for other than real estate loan	Can be a complex process
Finance companies	14-30%	1-3 years	$100,000+	An alternative when you don't have many	Expensive; picky about collateral
Banks	6-9%	1-5 years	50,000+	Generally least expensive	Generally hardest to qualify for
Venture Capital	24-40%	5-7 years	$500,000+	Can get large amounts	Very hard to get; share ownership

Resource Section

Updates, Discounts and a Complete List of Resources

Financing a business is a rapidly evolving arena. CorporateDirect. com strives to provide the most up to date information and special offers for our readers and clients. For a full list of discounts, resource links, coaching and current information please first visit: www.CorporateDirect.com/business-credit/

Starting and Maintaining Your Business

- Corporation, LLC and LP Formation: Form your entity the right way from the beginning to help attract financing opportunities.

  www.CorporateDirect.com or call 1-800-600-1760 (Mention this book and receive a discount.)

- Registered Agent Services: Every corporation, LLC, or LP must have a registered (or resident) agent to accept lawsuit notifications and official governmental notices in their state of formation and states where the company is qualified to do business. For registered agent services in all 50 states, please visit:

  www.corporatedirect.com/start-a-business/start-now/registered-agent-services/

- Corporate Clean Up: If your corporation or LLC is not up to date and needs to be cleaned up to avoid lawsuit vulnerabilities such as piercing the corporate veil, please visit:

  www.CorporateDirect.com/corporate-clean-up/

- Free Trademark Book: To receive a free book download entitled "Winning With Trademarks" please visit:

  www.CorporateDirect.com/asset-protection/winning-with-trademarks/

Lending Resources

- Association for Micro Enterprise Opportunity

  www.aeoworks.org/index.php/site/page/category/find

- California Association for Micro Enterprise Opportunity

  www.microbiz.org/cameo-membership/map-of-micro-lenders

- Community Development Financial Institutions
  www.cdfifund.gov/what_we_do/need_a_loan.asp

- Opportunity Finance Network
  Search for a CDFI near you at http://ofn.org/cdfi-locator

- Credit Unions
  www.ncua.gov

- State Loan Guarantee Programs: Under the State Small Business Credit Initiative (SSBCI) participating states can use $1.5 billion in federal funds for programs that leverage private lending to help finance small businesses and manufacturers that are creditworthy, but are not getting the loans they need to expand and create jobs.

  www.treasury.gov/resource-center/sb-programs/Pages/state-programs.aspx

- Grameen Bank is entering the market to create volume for very small loans under $5,000. www.grameenamerica.org

- Kiva funds loans under $10,000 in the U.S. through its crowd-funding platform. www.kiva.org

- Local Economic Development Programs
  - Many states have an organization devoted to local economic development. For example, the California Association for Local Economic Development (CALED) www.caled.org, is a collection of "public and private organizations and individuals involved in economic

development: the business of creating and retaining jobs." Micro-business increasingly is becoming a job creation strategy that local municipalities are formally embracing.

- o Search for "Economic Development Corporation" and "YOURCITY/COUNTY"

- For profit microlenders
  - o Lending Club and Prosper are funding borrowers with good credit.

    www.lendingclub.com, www.Prosper.com

  - o Progreso Financiero and Apoyo target the Latino market.

    www.progressfin.com/en, www.apoyofin.com

  - o Social network sites such as Kickstarter and Indie-a-go-go offer peer crowdfunding opportunities.

    www.kickstarter.com, www.indiegogo.com

    For a list of additional small business crowdfunding sites, visit CorporateDirect.com/business-credit

- Business Credit Cards

  Reviews of current business credit card offers are at CorporateDirect.com/business-credit/

Business Resources

- Micro Enterprise Development Programs

  www.aeoworks.org/index.php/site/page/category/find

  www.microbiz.org/cameo-membership/member-directory/

- Regional SBA office

  www.sba.gov/about-offices-list/3

- SCORE

  www.sba.gov/content/score-0

- Women's Business Centers

  www.sba.gov/content/women%E2%80%99s-business-centers

- The National Business Incubation Association

  www.nbia.org

- Double Digit Academy

  A fundraising intensive for women-owned businesses led by Julia Pimsleur (Chapter 14)

  www.DoubleDigitAcademy.com

- Ali Brown

  Resources for female entrepreneurs

  www.AliBrown.com

Additional Reading:

The State of Small Business Lending: Credit Access during the Recovery and How Technology May Change the Game. A whitepaper by Karen Gordon Mills and Brayden McCarthy, Harvard Business School

www.hbs.edu/faculty/Publication%20Files/15-004_09b1b-f8b-eb2a-4e63-9c4e-0374f770856f.pdf

The 1% of Business Funding: Venture Capital. This Kauffman Foundation Digest finds debt is the most common source of financing for new businesses, with about 40 percent of a business' initial startup capital coming from bank-financed debt. Equity is a less common form of initial funding, according to the Digest, with less than 3 percent of new firms funded by angel investors and less than 1 percent funded by venture capitalists. www.kauffman.org/newsroom/2015/06/debt-dominates-entrepreneurial-funding-vc-account-for-less-than-1-percent-of-financing.

INDEX

About the Authors

Garrett Sutton, Esq. is a nationally acclaimed corporate attorney and asset protection expert, who has sold more than 850,000 books guiding entrepreneurs and investors. Garrett's best sellers include: *Start Your Own Corporation, Run Your Own Corporation, The ABC's of Getting Out of Debt, Writing Winning Business Plans, Buying & Selling a Business* and *Loopholes of Real Estate* in Robert Kiyosaki's Rich Dad Advisor  series. He is also the author of *How to Use Limited Liability Companies & Limited Partnerships* and the co-author of *Finance Your Own Business.* Garrett enjoys helping entrepreneurs to succeed. He has over thirty years of experience in assisting individuals and businesses to determine their appropriate corporate structure, limit their liability, protect their assets and achieve their goals.

Garrett is the founder of Corporate Direct and Sutton Law Center, which since 1988 has provided affordable asset protection and corporate formation and maintenance services. His articles and quotes have been published in *The Wall Street Journal, New York Times,* CBS.com, Time.com and Credit.com. More information is found at www.CorporateDirect.com and www.sutlaw.com.

Gerri Detweiler is considered one of the nation's top credit experts. For more than two decades she has helped consumers find reliable answers to their credit questions. She has authored or coauthored five books, including *Reduce Debt, Reduce Stress: Real Life Solutions for Solving Your Credit Crisis, Deb Collection Answers: How to Use Debt Collection Laws to Protect Your Rights and In-*  *vest In Yourself: Six Secrets to A Rich Life.* Her syndicated personal finance columns for Credit.com appear on many leading news websites. She has also hosted a weekly personal finance radio show and over two hundred podcasts of these interviews are available at GerriDetweiler.com.

Gerri has been interviewed by the news media more than 3000 times including major outlets such as the New York Times, the Wall Street Journal and the Today Show. She has testified before Congress on consumer credit topics. Her goal is to simplify credit to help individuals and small business owners avoid costly traps and succeed financially.